D0005714

GO FOR IT!

GO FOR IT!

by Judy Zerafa

Workman Publishing, New York

Library of Congress Cataloging in Publication Data

Zerafa, Judy.
Go for it!

1. Youth—Conduct of life. 2. Success—Juvenile literature.
3. Goal (Psychology)—Juvenile literature.
I. Title.
BJ1661.Z37   1982   158   82-60065
ISBN 0-89480-213-5 (pbk.)

Cover and book design by Geoffrey Stevens

Workman Publishing Company, Inc.
708 Broadway
New York, N.Y. 10003

Manufactured in United States of America
First printing October 1982

20 19 18 17 16 15 14 13

Dedicated
with love
to my constant
and unfailing partners
and to
my parents

Acknowledgments:

To Tony Mattar, who turned on the light. To Nelson Carlo, Helen Gray, Jim Besaw, William Deardon, John Laird, Marilyn Hall, and David Hall for their assistance in the research for this book.

A very special thanks to Joan and Theron Raines for opening the door; for Candy Western for showing me the way; to Peter for taking the chance; to Sally for her endless patience, belief, guidance, and talent. To Donna, for always being there. To Paul, Jennifer, the Maureens, and Jim for their dedication and enthusiasm.

To Diane Glumb, Rolene Carpenter, and Dixie McGill for their many hours of typing.

To Deb Rodgers, Vicki, and T.P.; the S.F. Class of '85; Palastra Cheerleaders; T.C.S.H. IPR Class; and the CUM Youth Group.

To Mary Means and Donna Kuhar for a lifetime of love and support; and to Andy and Tom for the same reasons.

To Sandy Shaw for being such a special friend.

To my children: Marie, Ted, and Mary; my stepchildren: Matt, Carrie, and Ben . . . for all their encouragement, love, and suggestions.

And, most of all, to my husband, Richard, the center of my world; for his love, encouragement, and unfailing belief that I could do it!

Dear Friend:

Has anyone ever told you that you are an extraordinary human being and that you deserve—and can have—the best of everything? It's true! And there is no one who can keep you from becoming the person you want to be; no one who can prevent you from having the things that you want. No one, that is, except yourself.

Within you at this moment is a sleeping giant. It's called <u>potential</u>. Your potential is the combination of abilities and talents with which you were born. Researchers tell us that the average person uses only a small portion of his or her potential in an entire lifetime. That means that you can tap into an enormous resource of unused power—and this book will show you how.

With the talent and abilities that are already within you, and the help you will find in these pages, you will be able to achieve any goal. There is no reason for you to settle for second best. All you can ever dream of is within your grasp. All you have to do is <u>go for it.</u>!

Judy

Contents

Introduction

L ife is a journey, and each of us has a different amount of time in which to travel. To make the most of your journey, you will need the best in transportation.

If you think of life in this way, you can see for yourself that most people are not in the driver's seat. They are passengers, riding through the days of their lives while someone else sits at the wheel. They are not in control of their own destinies. They allow others to make their decisions. And they travel without maps; they just wander from place to place with no clear purpose.

Fewer than 10 percent of all people take control of their own lives and decide when and where they are going and how they will get there.

Your "car" was delivered the day you were born—custom-made and with its own set of tools. This book is an owner's manual for that car. With your tools and this manual, you have everything you need to chart your own course in life—and to make your journey exciting and worthwhile.

1

You Can Do Anything!

You can if you *think* you can! How many times have you heard that phrase? It's *true*. It doesn't matter how many other people believe in you—if you believe in yourself and think that you can accomplish a certain task or reach a particular goal—*you can!*

About ten years ago, two friends of mine were driving down a highway when a car in front of them went out of control, flew over an embankment, and landed upside down in a ditch. My friends stopped to see what they could do and found the driver pinned under the car. They couldn't tell whether she was dead or alive. It was late at night and there were no other cars on the road. They knew that they had to do something fast. Without thinking, the two of them moved the car with their own hands! It wasn't a little car, either. It was a luxury car, and weighed more than 4,000 pounds.

After the ordeal was over and the authorities were investigating the incident, my friends were asked how in the world they were able to move such a heavy car. They were both speechless—up until that point, they hadn't realized what they had done! They finally came to the conclusion that they had been able to move the car because they knew that they had *had* to move it or the woman inside the car would have died.

If these two people had been asked to move 4,000 pounds with their bare hands *before* the accident, it's almost certain that they would have laughed and said, "Don't be ridiculous, we *can't* do that!"

You will never know what you can do until you *try*. You can guess; you can imagine; and you can wonder. But you will *never know until you try*. If you are determined, if you hang in there and keep trying, and *if you think you can,* whatever it is you are working toward will be yours.

- Do you want a better life in the future than you've had up to now?
- Do you want to travel to foreign places?
- Do you want to be *very* popular?
- Would you like to be on the track team?
- Do you want to take a vacation with your friends?
- Would you like to be slim and lose the weight you keep telling yourself you need to lose?
- Do you want to own a car of your own?
- Would you like to buy a whole new wardrobe?
- Do you want an exciting, glamorous career?
- Do you want to be the best person you can be?

There is no trick or gimmick to achieving your goals and turning your dreams into reality. All you need is *determination* and *belief in yourself and in what you are doing*. The only barrier that can ever come between you and what you want is *not believing in yourself* and *giving up too soon*.

In each chapter of this book you will find stories about people who believed in themselves and who kept on trying until they reached what they were after. When you read their stories, you'll see that they each believed in themselves and in what they were doing; you will see that they were persistent and didn't give up.

Who are these people who can do anything?

They are people just like you. They are people of every race, color, and religion. They are short people, tall people, fat people, skinny people. They are people who are orphaned; people with two living parents; people whose parents were divorced; people whose parents are happily married. They are people who are raised by alcoholic parents and people who are raised by parents who never even held a glass of liquor. They are physically handicapped people; they are world-class athletes. They are people with learning disabilities; they are people with high IQs. *They are just people.*

Nelson Carlo is one of those people. He was born in a fishing village in Puerto Rico. His parents were divorced. He and his brother were raised by their grandmother until Nelson was nearly nine. At that time, the boys were sent to join their mother in a New York City ghetto. When Nelson was twelve, the three of them moved to Chicago.

Nelson hated school and spent more time in the principal's office than he did in class. When he was sixteen he quit school and worked in a grocery store until he was old enough to join the navy. He thought he would have an opportunity to see a lot of exotic ports around the world. Instead of enjoying his four years as he had planned, he disliked them even more than he had disliked school. There was even more authority in the service than there had been in school! If he hadn't been afraid of disgracing his mother, Nelson Carlo would have gone AWOL.

Even though his experience in the navy was not to his liking, Nelson learned one very important truth: you have to believe in yourself if you ever expect to accomplish anything. Before he was discharged, Nelson made up his mind that he wouldn't be one of life's losers.

When Nelson became a civilian again, he enrolled in an automotive mechanics school. He worked in a garage for a while and then opened his own shop. He was filled with enthusiasm and determination. He could fix anything! It didn't take him long to discover that there is more to owning an auto shop than knowing how to fix a car. He didn't know how to manage finances and, within a year, he lost $7,000 and his business.

Nelson felt he had lost a big battle, but not the war. His loss only made him *more* determined. Nearly a year later, he opened a gas station in partnership with a man who had a lot of business experience. The place was a success financially, but Nelson wasn't happy with the long hours. He sold his share of the partnership, knowing that he could find business success and personal satisfaction combined *if he kept looking*.

Nelson went to work for a large service organization. He was just another employee, plugging along, when he met a man who persuaded him to make an investment in a plan to manufacture long-handled dust pans for people who were handicapped.

The business failed, and this time Nelson lost $17,000! For most people, this setback would have been the end. But not for Nelson Carlo!

He next took a job as a salesman with a steel

distributor, even though the only thing he knew about steel was how to spell it. After three years of selling and learning about the business, he decided that he wanted to own his own steel company.

Nelson finally found the opportunity he wanted with a small specialty metals company. In order to take the job, he had to take a cut in pay. During the first year with this new company, Nelson increased its sales so much that he was able to start buying stock in the company. In a few years, he owned 45 percent of the company! Later, with the help of a small business loan, Nelson was able to buy the remaining stock, and at that point, *he owned the business!*

Nelson Carlo *believed in himself.* When the setbacks came (and they *always* do), he kept on going. He was determined to win!

Today Nelson Carlo is in his early forties. Last year his company made over $18 million! Not bad for a kid from a one-parent home, raised in the ghetto, and a high school dropout.

Economic history is filled with stories of businesses that suffered blow after blow of bad luck and financial setbacks before emerging as successful companies. There are examples in your own community. If you ask any successful businessperson in your town how his or her business grew, you will hear stories of struggle and persistence.

Don't be afraid to fail

E very time you hear about someone who has succeeded, you are hearing about someone who has failed, too. There is no such thing as a person who has never failed at anything.

If ever you start to feel that you might fall short of a goal, you might think about Abraham Lincoln. No one ever thinks of him as a failure. He wasn't always a winner, though. You've probably only heard about how he studied by firelight, became president of the United States, and freed the slaves. But there is another side to this very great man.

Did you know that he was fired from a job once? After that, he went into business for himself and went bankrupt. Did you know that he ran for elective office nine times before he finally won? Out of eleven elections, he only won two! Yet no one thinks of Lincoln as a loser!

History is filled with stories of scientists who would not give up until a cure was found for a specific problem. Louis Pasteur discovered a method of heating and cooling foods—specifically milk—to prevent the growth of harmful germs which prior to that time took the lives of thousands of people. His discovery—which we know as pasteurization—was not made overnight; it was the result of years of research, failure, more research and more failure, and finally success. Perhaps you are alive today because Pasteur would not give up.

Our libraries are filled with stories of people who have had one setback after another, but wouldn't stay down and out. People like Barbra Streisand. She didn't just decide to become a star and walk right into success. She tried over and over and over again to get someone to hire her as a singer. She knocked on hundreds of doors before one finally opened.

It is *not possible* for a person to be defeated if he or she keeps on trying. You *can't lose* if you keep picking yourself up each time life knocks you down. Within every single defeat or setback is a lesson to be learned or a skill to be mastered. Look for the lesson.

Pick yourself up and start over. If you try something and you lose, promise yourself you will try even harder the next time. Try with more enthusiasm than before. Picture yourself winning whatever it is you are after and give the next try all the enthusiasm and effort you can muster. If you lose again, repeat the procedure. If you lose ten times, repeat the procedure ten times. Keep on trying. Keep trying until you win! Don't let your failures poison your chances of winning; just say to yourself, "My last try was good training for this one."

When you hear about someone who has failed, you are also hearing about someone who has tried. You can never fail unless you try. There is no disgrace in failing. There is only disgrace in never having tried.

You can ... if you think you can

The next time you find yourself thinking that there is something that you just *can't* do, think about Roger Bannister. Roger Bannister was the first man to run a four-minute mile.

In 1886, a record was set by a man named Walker who ran the mile in 4:12 ¾. That record stood until 1923—thirty-seven years later—when Paavo Nurmi ran the mile in 4:10 ¾. He had shaved two whole seconds off Walker's record. Everyone in the world thought that Nurmi's accomplishment was unbelievable! "No one will ever be able to break his record," they said.

It took thirty-one more years for that record to be broken, and Roger Bannister did it. For the first time in history, a man ran a mile in four minutes flat.

Look what's happened since Bannister's record!

There have been scores of people who have broken the four-minute mile. Why?

Bannister was interviewed after his incredible accomplishment and everyone asked him whether or not he had special shoes, or if he ate any special foods, or if his training routine could account for his speed.

Bannister told the reporters that he didn't have special shoes, or anything else that one could actually see. He did have something special, though. He *believed* that it was possible for a human being to run a mile in four minutes. And that's exactly what he did!

Isn't it interesting that all of a sudden, so many people began running the mile in four minutes or less when it had taken thirty-one years for Bannister to surpass Nurmi? Once Bannister proved that it was possible, people stopped saying, "It can't be done!" Once a person stops saying "can't" and starts saying "*can*," it's a whole new game.

Keep one thing in mind, however: Roger Bannister didn't just get up one morning, put on a pair of sneakers, and say, "Today's the day, World!" Of course he didn't! He had to practice. He had to train. And he had to run a lot of races before he finally reached his goal.

▅▅▅

➠ YOU NEVER KNOW WHETHER OR NOT YOU CAN DO SOMETHING UNLESS YOU TRY.

➠ BELIEVE IN YOURSELF AND IN WHAT YOU ARE DOING.

➠ DON'T BE AFRAID OF FAILURE—EVERYBODY WHO TRIES FAILS SOMETIMES.

➠ KEEP A POSITIVE ATTITUDE AND KEEP TRYING UNTIL YOU ACHIEVE YOUR GOAL.

2

Attitude
Is
Everything

A ttitude is the way you think. Your attitude is something other people can actually see. They can hear it in your voice, see it in the way you move, feel it when they are with you. Your attitude expresses itself in everything you do, all the time, wherever you are.

Your attitude determines the direction in which your life goes. It's a little like driving your car. You can only drive a car in two directions: forward or backward. Your car can't move sideways; and it can't go up or down. Only forward and reverse. *A positive attitude will move your life forward; a negative attitude will put it in reverse.*

Other people may give you directions, but you are the driver, so it is you who will shift the gears. Do you want to spend your life moving ahead, or will you choose to spend your life backing up?

The course of your entire life will be decided by your attitude (or the direction in which you drive). Your attitude will decide how well you do in school. It will decide how you get along with your family and friends.

Your attitude will decide whether or not you discover your potential, develop your abilities, and reach your goals.

How can you develop a positive attitude?

You can develop a positive attitude by looking at every part of your life and seeing the difference between those things that you *can* control and those things that you can't control.

If you have a positive attitude, you are looking for ways to solve the problems that you can *solve, and you are letting go of the things over which you have no control.*

There will be times in your life when you have problems, even though you may be honestly maintaining a positive attitude; there will be times when you fail at whatever it is you are attempting, even though you are thinking positively. Failure does exist. Everyone fails at something once in a while, but you can *refuse* to dwell on failure and problems. You can *concentrate* on getting the best results from the worst conditions.

You can develop a positive attitude by recognizing that there will be both good and bad in your life and deciding to emphasize the *good* over the bad. When you do this, you will see that the good *increases*. If you concentrate on the bad, you will see that the unhappiness and failure increases.

There was a young boy who lived in the town where I grew up. His name was Bill. Bill would come home from school each day, throw his books on his bed, change his clothes, and race outside to find someone with whom he could play. Bill loved to play all kinds of games—baseball, football, basketball, soccer. When the weather turned cold, Bill would go skating on a nearby pond where a group of his friends got together and learned to play hockey.

Bill loved life, and he had a lot of friends. When he entered high school, he tried out for all kinds of sports, and he made most of the teams. He was truly an all-around athlete. In his junior year, he lettered in three sports: football, basketball, and track.

At the start of his senior year, Bill was in a terrible car accident. He lost both of his legs. He was in the hospital for months. Everyone felt very sorry for Bill because they knew that he would never again be able to play any of the games he loved so much. Most people thought that Bill's life was over before it had really begun. Bill had been so good in sports that there is little doubt that he would have gotten a scholarship to college because of his athletic ability.

During his long months of recovery, Bill studied hard to try and catch up on the time he was missing in school, but he could only study just so many hours a day and then his mind became too tired to concentrate. He began to relax his mind by doodling on a pad of paper. He would draw simple pictures to fill up the time and to keep his mind off the fact that he would rather have been outside with the other kids.

Bill missed nearly a whole year of school, but he was eventually able to return to classes in a special wheelchair. Beginning his senior year again, he decided to take an art course. In a very short time, he was getting A's in this class; Bill had never before gotten an A in his life. His work was so good that one of his teachers took some of his paintings and drawings to a group of local artists for their opinion. The artists liked the work so much that they decided to ask Bill if he would want to exhibit at a local art fair.

Bill did show some of his paintings, and before long gained quite a reputation. He began making money from the things he did with his hands and his head. In fact, using his talent, he was able to earn enough money to put himself through college.

Bill now makes a fortune from his paintings. He has a wife and family and loves his life and his work. Bill *made his own decision to think positively;* to make the best of a bad situation, to live and accomplish something that was under his control. It would have been easy for him to spend the rest of his life blaming a careless driver for taking away his legs . . . but what would that have gotten him? What good would bitterness have done for Bill?

If Bill had been able to continue at sports, he might never have discovered that he had any artistic talent. He might have gone through college as an athlete and perhaps ended up on a professional team. Bill feels that his ability to paint and earn a living in this way will last for many years and will give him much more satisfaction than he would have been able to get from work as an athlete.

If Bill had the choice of having two good legs, of course he would choose to have them. He doesn't have that choice, so he has chosen to make the best of what he does have.

You can develop a positive attitude by emphasizing the good, by being tough-minded, and by refusing defeat.

Your attitude works like a magnet

We all know that magnets attract some things and not others—most metal objects will simply leap at a magnet if the magnet is strong enough, but wood, paper, rubber, and so forth will not react at all. It is almost as if the metal recognizes something in the magnet that forces it to respond.

Take a look around you in school. Have you ever noticed how the most popular kids in class stick together? They do that because they possess similar qualities; they have outgoing personalities. The same thing is true of any group of people. The people with similar interests tend to find one another no matter how large the class, the school, or the community. Those who are interested in many things have many friends. Those who have few interests have few friends.

Take a good look around your city or town. You'll see that some parts of town are nice and clean, with well-kept houses and yards. Other parts are filthy, with dilapidated houses and yards overgrown with weeds.

The sections that are dirty and run-down don't have to look that way, but the people who live in those areas don't care how their houses look. They don't fix things that break, or clean things that get dirty; they don't put any effort into anything. People who live there *don't care how their houses look,* and these neighborhoods tend to draw people of that same type.

The people who live in the sections where everything is neat and clean *do* care about how their places look. They repair things and keep things clean. They make an effort. Likewise, these areas attract others *who care about themselves and the environment in which they live.*

If people who take care of their homes (and themselves) find themselves in a run-down section, it doesn't take them long to find a way to get into a different neighborhood.

Another example right in your school is the way people dress and take care of themselves. I'm not talking about expensive clothes; I'm talking about being clean and neat. Do you ever see a well-groomed person— one who always has clean hands and face and clean, well-pressed clothes—becoming friends with someone who always wears filthy clothes and has body odor, dirty hair, and grimy hands and face? Never! The messy, unkempt kids always stick together, just as the well-groomed ones do.

Let's think about our magnet again. If you take a magnet and hold it over a paper clip, the paper clip will jump up to meet the magnet. Now hold that paper clip close to another paper clip. What happens? The second paper clip attaches itself to the first paper clip. But if you hold the first paper clip over a rubber band, the rubber band won't be attracted to the paper clip no matter how close the two get. *Any object that is attracted by a magnet becomes a magnet itself as long as it remains in contact with the real magnet.*

Look for friendships with those who are involved in life! Listen for "I can!" "Let me do it!" "Let's try it this way." Surround yourself with these people and you will be more likely to maintain a positive attitude.

Positive attitude and negative attitude are both magnets. They attract the same thing.

Positive attitudes always invite positive results. Negative attitudes always invite negative results.

Attitude makes a difference every hour, every day, in everything that you do for your entire life. What you get out of each thing you do *will equal the attitude you have when you do it.*

Anything that you do with a positive attitude will work *for* you. Anything that you do with a negative attitude will work *against* you.

➠ YOUR ATTITUDE IS THE *WAY* YOU THINK.

➠ DEVELOP A POSITIVE ATTITUDE BY REFUSING DEFEAT AND MAKING THE MOST OF WHAT YOU HAVE.

➠ YOUR ATTITUDE IS LIKE A MAGNET.

➠ YOUR ATTITUDE IS THE MOST IMPORTANT THING ABOUT YOU.

➠ THE RESULTS OF WHAT YOU DO ARE IN DIRECT RELATIONSHIP TO THE ATTITUDE YOU HAVE WHEN YOU DO IT.

➠ WITH A POSITIVE ATTITUDE, YOU CAN DO ANYTHING!

3

Image Is More Than Skin Deep

Your image isn't just one thing. It's a composite, or a combination of many things. Your image is made up of your physical appearance, the way you talk, your attitude, the way you move your body, and personal hygiene and body care.

The most important part of your image is your *attitude*. It is so important that we've devoted an entire chapter to it. You may be surprised to learn that your looks—that is, the way your physical characteristics are put together—are the *least* important aspect of your image. That's pretty good news when you consider that your looks are the part of your image over which you have the *least* control!

Your looks are just like the outside of a package— the gift wrapping. Looks cover the important part of you—the part that is inside. When you open a present, the wrapping paper is almost forgotten in the excitement of discovering what is in the package, right? *It is exactly the same with you.* Your value is within you. *It isn't the way you look that will decide your life and your future. It is what you develop on the inside that counts.*

The next time you watch television, take a good look at the national and world leaders. Study the faces and the shapes of business leaders, well-known scientists, and social leaders. Most of us think of these people as the "beautiful people." If you take a careful look, you will see that many of them are far from perfect looking. They have physical imperfections the same as you and I.

Glance through your history books and leaf through a couple of magazines. You'll see pictures of famous, successful, happy people who are *very* plain looking. There are some fat ones, some short ones, and some bald ones; some with crooked teeth, and others with long noses or hooked noses. Some have droopy chins; others have no chins. Some have eyes that are too close together; others have eyes that are too far apart.

See what I mean?

The people who play the parts in your favorite television shows and movies aren't all perfect looking either, are they? Because the people on television, in the movies, and in newspapers and magazines are the so-called "important people," we look at them through rose-colored glasses. We *think* of them as important, and we overlook their physical imperfections. When we consider these people, we see their *total image,* not just their facial features and the shape of their bodies.

Which would you rather own: a car with the body of a Rolls-Royce that houses a lawn mower engine, the suspension system from a baby carriage and the battery from a flashlight; or a car with the body of a Chevy that houses a Mercedes engine, the chassis of a Porsche, and the power system of a Cadillac? There's no question which you will choose, is there? The car that *looks* like a Rolls-Royce certainly won't get you very far. It will rattle, make all kinds of terrible noises, and it will stall—if, indeed, you can ever get it to run at all. But the plain-looking Chevy with the best of everything under the hood will take you anywhere you want to go.

Whether you were born beautiful or handsome, average or plain, it doesn't matter. You can achieve a beautiful or handsome image by concentrating on the more important aspects of your *total* image.

The way you talk is important to your image

If you don't use your voice in a pleasant manner, or if you don't have command of the language, your image will be a weak one—and a weak image makes you easy to forget. On the other hand, if you know how to use your voice and language properly, you will be able to create an impression of strength, charm, intelligence, leadership, and sophistication.

The way you talk will have a great effect on whom you will have as friends; the grades you will receive in school; the way you get along with others; the employment you find; the salary you make; the influence you have with your own family; and the position you hold in your community. *Learning to talk well is important to every aspect of your life.*

You can't hide the way you talk. Once you open your mouth, the whole world knows! *The image you create and carry with you throughout life is closely connected to the way you talk.*

It's Thursday night and a boy we'll call Joe has

just come home from a week's vacation with his family. As soon as Joe gets inside the house, he heads for the phone to find out what's been happening while he has been away. He calls his best friend Mark.

"Hi, Mark. Just got back! What's happening?"

"Hi, Joe! Not much, but you did get back in time for Kathy's party Saturday night. Everybody's gonna be there."

"Oh, great. That means everybody but me has a date by now."

"Good news. My aunt and uncle from Seattle are coming tomorrow and they're bringing my cousin Jenny who's just our age."

"Mark, you and I made a pact about blind dates, remember?"

"Yeah. I remember. But I've got a picture of Jenny, and you'll want to forget the pact after you see it."

The next day Mark showed Joe the picture. Joe couldn't believe his good luck. I'll have the best-looking date at the party! Joe said to himself.

On Saturday night, Joe went over to Mark's house to pick up Jenny and Mark. When Joe rang the doorbell, it took Mark a long time to answer.

"Hey, buddy! Is everybody ready?" Joe asked enthusiastically.

"Yeah. Almost," Mark replied weakly.

After a few seconds, Joe became suspicious. "Mark, what's up?" he said under his breath. "Jenny didn't come after all, is that it?"

"No, Joe, Jenny's here. She'll be down in a minute."

"Mark, something's wrong! Don't tell me—she gained a hundred pounds."

"No, Joe. Honest! It's . . ."

Just then Mark's mother and Jenny came down the

stairs. Joe was so confused he didn't know what to think. There wasn't anything wrong with Jenny! He turned to Mark and said under his breath, "You had me scared stiff for a second. She's fantastic!" Joe couldn't believe his good fortune.

Mark, pulling himself together, said, "Jenny, I'd like you to meet my friend Joe. Joe, this is my cousin Jenny."

Joe looked at Jenny, and after a moment he stammered, "Hi . . . Jenny."

Then, Jenny opened her beautiful mouth and in the most *incredibly* squeaky voice said, "Ain't Mark jest a doll fer gettin' us tagether!"

Joe's heart stopped. *She can't talk!* Joe thought. *She looks like an angel, but she sounds like a dying pig! Mark, old buddy, I'll get you for this if it takes all year,* he silently vowed.

How do you think Joe pictured Jenny after that? He was embarrassed to be with her. All he could think of that evening was how he could keep her from talking to his friends. Needless to say, he avoided going near Mark's house for the remainder of her two-week visit.

Whether you are on a date, in class, at a club meeting, with your friends, or anywhere, if the way you talk is poor it doesn't matter how good your ideas are, how profound your thoughts, or how intense your feelings. *The weaker your ability to communicate verbally, the less seriously anyone will consider what you say.*

How you can improve the way you talk

If you feel that you are not a confident speaker, or that you are dissatisfied with the way you talk, you can do something about it. Just follow these suggestions.

1. *Practice enunciating.* Make sure you open your mouth wide enough to get the words out; use your tongue and your lips. Find someone to practice with, and try lip reading—"talking" without making any sounds.

2. *Listen to educated people.* Learn new words from them; learn pronunciation from them; learn articulation from them. But this doesn't mean mimicking them. You can speak well and correctly and still speak with *your own style.* Just like everything else about you, your manner of speaking is unique. There isn't anyone else in the world with the same facial and mouth construction as you; therefore, there isn't anyone else in the world who can *naturally* sound just like you. Your voice should have its own identity. Incorporate everything you learn into your own special way of speaking. *Be yourself* when you speak.

3. *Change the rhythm of your speech.* Listen to your favorite D.J. and to news broadcasters on radio and television. Notice how they place emphasis on different words.

4. *Pronounce all words correctly.* You may have heard people say lie-berry when they mean lie-brar-ee (library), guv-ment when they mean gov-ern-ment (government), prob-lee when they mean prob-ab-lee (probably), en-vyre-munt when they mean en-vye-ern-ment (environment), ex-pesh-lee when they mean es-pesh-al-lee (especially), ar-tik when they mean ark-tik (Arctic). Get yourself a good dictionary, learn the pronunciation guide (it's easier than you might think), and pay attention to how words are properly pronounced.

5. *Read aloud for at least ten minutes a day.* Reading aloud will improve your sentence structure, your speech, and your vocabulary. In addition, of course,

It's All in the *Emphasis*

TO SEE HOW EMPHASIS works, read the following sentence aloud, emphasizing the capitalized word:

> THIS is a great day.
> This IS a great day.
> This is A great day.
> This is a GREAT day.
> This is a great DAY.

YOU CAN SEE HOW shifting the stress changes the meaning.

READ THE NEWSPAPER aloud, emphasizing a word here and there. Read your schoolwork the same way. You can even practice on a grocery list! When you talk to your family and friends, practice placing emphasis on a word here and there. Who knows? You may become the next big name on your favorite radio station!

you will accumulate knowledge. *We remember more of what we hear* and *read than what we only read*. The more of your senses—hearing, seeing, smelling, touching, and tasting—you can involve in any learning experience, the greater the impact on your ability to retain that knowledge.

6. *Wear a pleasant expression on your face* to have

a pleasant voice. If your face is all screwed up in anger, your voice comes up through your throat sounding like anger. If you have sad, droopy eyes, your voice comes out sad and droopy. If you knit your brows together, your voice comes out sounding worried. If you throw your head back and stick out your chin, you sound tough. But when you smile, you can't help sounding sunny and pleasant. When your eyes dance and your smile sparkles, you can find an audience *anywhere*. Think of your smile as your own little personal magnet!

7. *Be willing to participate more in conversation.* When you are at home with your family, talk with them. It's easy to fall into a routine of just making statements and asking questions. Be interested in what others have to say. *Being interested is the best way to stimulate a conversation.*

8. *Speak slowly* enough so that each word is distinct. Don'trunyourwordstogether.

9. *Don't interrupt.* The only time you should ever break this rule is if the building you are in is on fire or there is a medical emergency.

10. *Don't repeat.* Say what you have to say and stop.

What will the results be if I improve the way I speak?

The way you talk will greatly influence whether or not you get what it is you're looking for—today, tomorrow, and later in your life. Talk isn't cheap, but thank heavens you can afford it! The price is *time* and *effort—your* time and *your* effort. The more time and effort you spend on learning to talk well, *the better you will talk*. The better you talk, the *more you will be able to influence people*. The more you influence people, the *more you will get them to do what you want*. When you get them to do what you want, *you're the leader*. When you're the leader, *you make the rules*. When you make the rules, *you are in charge*.

Your body speaks a language all its own

You can usually tell by the way they move whether people are happy or troubled, confident or unsure of themselves. To create a confident image, here are some pointers.

Do walk a little faster than you are used to walking. This creates the image that you are a person with a purpose. It lets others know that you *know* where you are going. *Don't* shuffle your feet as you walk. This makes you look uncertain and lost.

Do keep your head held high and your eyes focused before you. *Don't* lower your head and look down at the ground. This makes you look as though you are afraid.

Do throw your shoulders back comfortably and tilt your chin up. This gives your whole body a lift. Imagine that there is an invisible string attached to your chest; then pretend that there is someone on the other end pulling the string upward. That's the way you should stand. Be sure to keep your chin up and you'll find that you actually breathe easier this way, too. *Don't* hunch your shoulders and let your chin drop. This makes your body look heavy, and that makes you look tired, lacking in enthusiasm. Bad posture also gives you an overall look of being a submissive person (someone afraid to stand up for his or her rights); someone people can take advantage of easily. You don't *ever* want people to feel that way about *you!*

Do keep the corners of your mouth tilted up. This puts a sparkle in your eyes and makes your face an exciting one. With your mouth tilted up, that invisible string attached to your chest will stay taut and you will find it easy to keep those shoulders back and chin up. People will see you as a person with a "sunny" personality and will be drawn to you because of a feeling of warmth and trust. *Don't* frown. Ever.

Do look people in the eye when you talk to them. Eye contact forces a person to focus on you and what you are saying. *Don't* look away from the person to whom you are speaking. Shifting your eyes away from someone can destroy the credibility of what you are saying. Shifty eyes are equated with dishonesty.

Do look your best at all times, even when you are by yourself. *Don't* let anyone see you with an unwashed face, uncombed hair, or in dirty clothes. It's just not the image for you.

The way you care for your body tells people how you feel about yourself

A clean body, shiny hair, white teeth, cared-for hands, and a firm physique makes a strong statement about a person. And so does a body with greasy skin, dull hair, stained teeth, torn fingernails, and flabby muscles.

The way your body looks is entirely up to you. You are born with a genetic heritage that endows you with certain physical features. These you cannot change . . . but the way you present them to the rest of the world is up to you.

Do you know anyone who eats a lot of junk—candy, ice cream, pastry, soft drinks, or fried and salty food? This type of food leaves its mark. Muscle tone is poor; skin is loose and soft. Salt causes the body to retain fluid, and too much of it makes the skin look puffy. And these are only the *visible* signs of junk food! The problems that these foods cause in your insides can be far more serious.

What you eat is converted into the energy needed by your brain and other vital organs. Your body was designed to function at its peak on specific types of food, such as vegetables, fruit, grain, lean meat, fish, cheese, and milk products. In addition to these, it is also necessary to drink plenty of water each day to flush normal toxins from the body.

But it isn't enough to just eat properly. To keep that body of yours in good shape, you have to exercise. If you are young and have a good physique, you can keep it through daily exercise and a healthful diet. If your body has gotten out of shape, exercise and diet will reclaim it.

You are never too young or too old to begin taking good care of yourself. It should become a habit.

At the beginning of this chapter, we said that your total image is a composite of five things: attitude, the way you talk, body language, body care and hygiene, and finally, physical appearance. By now you can see how each of these parts fit together to create the total image. *If you stress the first parts, people will see the physical image you want them to see.*

⟹ YOUR IMAGE IS MUCH MORE THAN YOUR PHYSICAL CHARACTERISTICS.

⟹ THE WAY YOU TALK IS IMPORTANT TO YOUR IMAGE.

⟹ GOOD HEALTH AND HYGIENE HABITS WILL STAY WITH YOU FOREVER.

⟹ YOUR BODY HAS A LANGUAGE ALL ITS OWN.

4

The Arch
of Triumph

The most successful and fantastic relationships between people are based on four attributes: appreciation, responsibility, courtesy, and honesty. Perhaps it would be helpful for you to remember that the first letters of these attributes spell the word *arch*. I call this the Arch of Triumph. Just as Napoleon built the Arc de Triomphe in Paris to commemorate his successes, you can build your triumphal arch to help you attain fantastic relationships.

Before actors go on stage to perform in front of an audience, they rehearse each scene over and over. Before the hometown team takes to the road for competition, they practice their plays again and again. Before you are ready to drive on the busy highway, you have to practice; you practice in parking lots and side streets before you can take on the freeway. And before you can expect to master the art of successful relationships in society, you need to sharpen these skills also. What better place to learn the foundation for these fantastic relationships than in your own home?

Developing and maintaining satisfying and rewarding relationships with your family is far more difficult than doing the same thing with people who live apart from you. Why is this? you ask. The answer is simply: "Familiarity breeds contempt." This old expression means that it is easy to forget that those with whom you live day in and day out are people with feelings and needs that are the same as yours. Because it is harder to be appreciative, responsible, courteous, and honest— remember the arch you want to build—at home, developing these habits within your family unit will make them much stronger in your social, school, and business life.

But the best part of starting to build your arch at home is that those who are on the receiving end of your appreciation, responsibility, courtesy, and honesty will respond in new and different ways. You will automatically be given more freedom and more time to do what you want to do; your parents will begin saying yes more often.

Showing your appreciation for others will make you rich in pleasure

What feels better than being told that you're terrific? Or being told that you have done something very well? Or being told that someone is proud of you? There aren't many things that can make you feel better than knowing someone else appreciates you and your abilities. The only feeling even close to that is the feeling you get from knowing that *you* have made someone else feel that way.

Put the stone of appreciation in your Arch of Triumph

by practicing around the house. And if you can show your appreciation or gratitude in *creative* ways, ways that use your *imagination,* it will be remembered longer than words.

Not too long ago, Rosemary's mother came down with the flu and had to stay in bed for a couple of days. Because they lived close to school, Rosemary was able to come home at lunchtime and fix her mother something to eat so she wouldn't have to get out of bed.

One day Rosemary fixed a plate of cold cuts and cheese. She cut both the meat and the cheese in small pieces and arranged them in the design of a smiley face. On the napkin she wrote, "The smiley face is me saying thank you for all the times you took care of me when I didn't feel well." It only took a few extra minutes for Rosemary to fix a lunch that her mother would always remember.

Monica was always asking her fifteen-year-old son to turn his clothes right side out before he threw them into the laundry hamper. She kept telling him that it would only take him a second to perform this little courtesy that would save her time and aggravation.

One day while Monica was facing a particularly high mountain in laundry-land, she found still another pair of her son's socks turned wrong side out and in a kind of ball. As she turned them, a piece of paper fell out of one of the socks. It read, "If I had left this one right side out, you wouldn't have found my note. I just want to let you know that I've submitted your name for the Hall of Fame under the category of Best Mother Who Ever Lived."

While Ted was emptying the wastepaper baskets one day, he found a note taped to the bottom of the basket in his sister's room. She had drawn a picture of a stick person with a message that read "If it weren't for you, I'd be up to my neck in debris!"

How creative are you? You can have a lot of fun doing things like this. Start with your family and branch out. You're in for some very good feelings when you see how much your appreciation and creativity mean to the people who touch and share your life.

Assuming responsibility will make you rich in opportunities

M any people are afraid of the word *responsibility.* They think that it means "obligation" and "worry" and "pressure" and "being tied down." It actually means just the opposite. When people realize that you are a responsible person you will find that they respond by giving you more privileges, more choices, and *more control over your own life.*

Start cementing your stone of responsibility into position by *demonstrating* that you are responsible for yourself, the things that belong to you, and the obligations that are yours. Once you assume these kinds of responsibility, people will learn to count on you. Your parents and others will know that they can trust you, and you will be given new opportunities around the home, in school, and in your community.

To better understand how your parents will react to your development of responsibility for your belongings and obligations, consider the following:

Imagine that *you* are asked to care for two people for a week who are younger than yourself. It will be up to you to make all the decisions concerning their activities while they are in your care.

Jim and John are twins; both are in school. When they come home in the afternoon, Jim throws his books and jacket on the nearest available piece of furniture and heads for the backyard after a short detour to the refrigerator. John, on the other hand, hangs up his jacket and takes his books to his room. While there, John changes his clothes, puts on jeans and sneakers, and *then* makes a pass at the fridge on his way out to the yard.

When it's time for dinner, you call the two boys in to get cleaned up and come to the table. Jim drops his baseball and mitt on the ground and runs into the house. As he races through the living room, his shoes leave marks across the carpeting. But he does get to the table first!

John takes the softball bat he was using and puts it in its place in the garage. He pulls off his sneakers as he comes into the house and *then* he heads for the dining room. (John arrives at the table only seconds behind Jim.)

After dinner, you begin to clear the table and Jim heads for the television set. John carries his own plate and silverware to the sink. You have to ask Jim to come back and do the same.

On the second day, both boys come home from school and tell you that they have to collect leaves from six different kinds of trees for a science project due at the end of the week. You suggest that they do it this afternoon because they have a hockey game tomorrow. After hearing both boys grumble because it's such a nice day and they would rather play ball, John decides that he will go look for the leaves. Jim sits at the kitchen table eating cookies and telling you all about a great new game he saw in a magazine. When you are busy doing something else and *think* that Jim is out looking for his leaves, he is really in the living room, watching television.

Before they go to bed, you ask them to take their hockey uniforms to the laundry room so that you can wash them before their game tomorrow night.

After they leave for school the next day, you discover that John's uniform is in the laundry room where it is supposed to be, but you can't find Jim's. You have to go to the boys' room and search for it. You find it on the floor underneath the good sweater his aunt and uncle gave him for his birthday. Besides finding his clothes on the floor, you also see that his bed hasn't been made. John's bed has been made and although there are some things that aren't where they should be, his clothes are put away.

On the fourth morning, you hear Jim asking John if he can have some of the leaves that John collected for the science project that is due today. John tells him that he only has enough for his own assignment, and Jim starts to moan that if John doesn't give him some, he will receive a bad grade and the teacher will scold him.

After the boys depart for school, a neighbor lady calls you to say that she and her family are planning to be out of town for two weeks and would like to hire one of the boys to feed and water their dog and to take their mail in each day. For doing these jobs, she will pay $15. The neighbor asks you to decide which of the twins gets the job.

Would it be difficult for you to decide?

Of course not. You know which twin deserves the job. John showed that he was responsible for himself, for his possessions, for his obligations, and that he could be trusted—and counted on—to look after the neighbor's dog and mail.

It's easy to become a more responsible person and to earn your parents' respect. *Do more than you are doing now.* And, *do it better.* If you learn to do these things at home, you will be a responsible person for the rest of your life—and opportunities that will enrich your life will keep on coming your way.

Displaying courtesy will make you rich in respect

E veryone likes being treated courteously, but a lot of people think courtesy is a superfluous "luxury item"—a lot of nice words and gestures that don't mean anything. That is not true. When you are courteous to people, they do more than just like it; they remember it and respect you for it. They will see you as more than just a "well-mannered person"; they will tend to listen to your opinions more, they will like you better, and they will certainly treat you with respect.

You may already have a very good relationship with your family. Or, you may have a terrible one. Perhaps you fall somewhere in between. No matter how good, bad, or in-between things are at home, a courteous attitude will make your life happier. No family relationship is so great that it can't be better; no family relationship is so bad that it can't be improved.

A sure way to become a courteous person is to pretend that *you* are the host or hostess when you are with others. Make believe that everyone with whom you come in contact during the day is your guest—*includ-*

ing the members of your family!

A sensational host is very interested in what his guests say and do. He or she is concerned about the way they feel. He or she encourages them and their ideas. He or she makes them feel *special*. If you treat people like special guests—with courtesy and kindness—99 times out of 100, they will treat you that way in return.

Being honest will make you rich in trust

O f the four stones in your arch, the most important is honesty. The first three are more like social graces, but honesty should be a way of life. If you occasionally fail to express your appreciation, if you temporarily lapse in a particular responsibility, or if somewhere along the way your manners slip, you will be forgiven by your fellow man. But being dishonest even once can make you suspect for a lifetime.

Honesty is more than telling the truth. Honesty is never taking something that doesn't belong to you— even an ashtray or towel from a hotel. Honesty means never cheating—even if it means that you will not do well on a test. Honesty means never gossiping, because it might harm the reputation of another person, and taking the good name of another person is stealing. Honesty is never stretching the truth to keep yourself out of trouble. Honesty means being fair—looking at an issue or cause from every side. Honesty means never having ulterior motives when you do something—like making friends with someone you don't really like just so you can meet that person's brother or sister. Honesty means never concealing the truth—remember the

How to Have a Better Relationship with Your Family

WHEN YOU GET UP in the morning, put on your best smile before you leave your room. Instead of grumbling at everyone as you get ready for school, work, or whatever you have planned for the day, take the time to say "good morning" with that bright smile of yours. (I have to warn you, though: if being pleasant to your family hasn't been part of your nature up to now, everyone will probably wonder what you're up to!)

IF YOU HAVE BREAKFAST with your family, ask everyone what they plan to do with their day. *Be interested.* (On day one, they may not be able to answer you. They will probably be in shock.)

DO YOU REMEMBER how good you felt the last time someone took the time to ask you what happened to you during the day? Listen carefully to what everyone in your family has to say. You will probably be surprised to discover that in addition to being members of your family, these people are *interesting*.

KEEP UP THE PRACTICE of meeting your family on friendly terms for the next seven days. You'll be very surprised by their reactions . . . and you'll also find that after a week, you won't have to *think* about how to act or what to say—it will become automatic. It will have become a habit.

Watergate scandal? Honesty means not wasting the time for which your boss is paying you. Honesty means keeping your promises. Honesty means being a sincere person, not a phony. Oh yes, honesty is much, much more than telling the truth.

Consider how you would feel if you discovered that someone you know had been dishonest with you. The dishonesty might have been a small one, and maybe you had been friendly with that person for a long time. But from then on, you would always wonder if he or she was trustworthy.

Because honesty is a way of life, it effects all we think and everything we do. Your honesty determines your values or moral standards. Do you cheat on tests? Do you stretch the truth when you think you can stay out of trouble by doing so? Do you ever reason that because "everybody" does something, that it isn't wrong? Then you're not being honest—with others or with yourself.

Being honest is the only way you can win trust, loyalty, respect, and admiration.

⏺⏺⏺⏺

➠ THE BEST WAY TO LEARN HOW TO BUILD GOOD RELATIONSHIPS IS TO START LEARNING AT HOME.

➠ WHEN YOU USE YOUR HOME AS A TRAINING GROUND TO LEARN ABOUT RELATIONSHIPS, YOUR HOME LIFE WILL BE HAPPIER AND YOUR PARENTS WILL GIVE YOU MORE FREEDOM.

➠ WHEN YOU BECOME A MORE APPRECIATIVE, RESPONSIBLE, COURTEOUS, AND HONEST PERSON, YOU WILL HAVE MORE CONTROL OVER YOUR LIFE.

➠ WHATEVER YOU GIVE IN APPRECIATION, RESPONSIBILITY, COURTESY, AND HONESTY, YOU WILL GET BACK MANY TIMES OVER.

➠ YOU CAN LOOK FORWARD TO STEPPING THROUGH YOUR ARCH OF TRIUMPH TO A FUTURE FILLED WITH FANTASTIC RELATIONSHIPS.

5

Use Your Imagination

There is nothing in all the world as incredible as your mind. In fact, scientists figure that to build a machine that would do everything your mind is capable of doing they would have to spend over *three billion* dollars! Can you imagine? Three billion dollars!

You have the original of this fabulous piece of equipment. You own it outright. But do you know how to use it? Do you know all that it is capable of doing?

Let's see how the mind works. Think of your mind as having four compartments. Each one can be thought of as a cylinder in the motor of your "machine."

Cylinder No. 1 generates the power to absorb information. Our minds absorb information through our senses of sight, sound, smell, taste, and touch.

Cylinder No. 2 generates the power to retain. This means that the information coming to us from the first compartment is being classified, filed, and stored for future use.

Cylinder No. 3 generates the power to judge. This is the compartment that makes decisions. It weighs the facts and gives us our decisions based on the information available. (The more work that compartments 1 and 2 do, the better this compartment will work.)

Cylinder No. 4 generates the power of imagination, the highest power of the mind. This is the power that moves civilization forward and brings about social, scientific, and technological progress.

Most of us use the first three switches on a regular basis. In fact, the first three powers are present in all animals—not to as high a degree as they are in human beings, but there nevertheless. Your pet dog, for example, can absorb information through his senses. Using his sense of smell, he can find a piece of meat that you might have hidden. Your dog retains information. After his first encounter with a steak bone, he knows what it smells like, and if there's one around, he'll find it! To a degree, your dog also has the power to make judgments, too. If he does something you don't want him to do and you punish him for it, he will soon avoid doing it again, because he has figured out what will happen if he does.

But there is no way that dogs, cats, horses, or any other pets can develop their imagination, because their minds don't have that power.

Everything you will ever have or will achieve depends on the way you decide to use your mind.

How can you develop more imagination?

You can develop your imagination by *using it*. To keep any part of your body in good working order, it has to be *used*. Your legs, for example, will quit working if you stop using them. They will become wobbly, and you will walk funny. If you don't use them for a couple of months, you won't even be able to stand on them. But if you start exercising them regularly, they will soon be back to full strength again. And if you keep it up, you can develop them even further.

Your imagination works exactly the same way! If you don't use it, it eventually dries up. But, if you use it every day, it increases in ability and strength. Here are ten exercises to strengthen your imagination:

1. When you're in class or listening to a speaker, write down questions or ideas that come to you while you're listening.

2. When you look at something, really *look* to see what makes it work; really watch what is happening.

3. Ask yourself questions like: "Why am I doing this?" or "How can I improve what I'm doing?"

4. Try to figure out better ways of doing the things you do.

5. Spend a part of every day increasing your knowledge.

6. Make time in each day to just plain *think*.

7. *Listen* to other people's ideas.

8. Add your own ideas to those of others.

9. Before you make decisions, try to *get all the facts*.

10. Ask a lot of questions. (I'm talking about questions that require more than yes or no for an answer.)

What kinds of things will come out of my imagination once I develop the power?

*E*verything you see around you that is manmade, and every fantastic accomplishment about which you have read was once just an idea in someone's mind. Everywhere you look, you see the miracles that have come from the imagination.

Your television set was no more than a dream fifty years ago, but has influenced our lives more in the past fifty years than man has been influenced since the beginning of time. And TV came about because of man's imagination.

Your bicycle was once just an idea in someone's imagination. The pavement that makes our highways, driveways, and sidewalks was once just an idea in someone's imagination too. Even the toys you played with as a young child are examples of the products of human imagination.

There have been many studies done on the lives of creative people. These are the people who have given us the advances in science, technology, and sociology. The following list of questions is based on the characteristics found in these people. Not all of the characteristics were found in each and every one of these people, but many of them were. Ask yourself the questions to see how many of these traits you possess.

1. Do you have the desire to work long and hard?

2. Do you have the courage to hang on and fight for what you believe in?

3. Do you have definite goals?

4. Do you look for new opportunities and new answers to old questions?

5. Do you have a desire to know more and a willingness to learn?

6. Do you have physical and mental fitness (good health and a positive attitude)?

7. Do you have a sense of honesty and integrity?

8. Do you listen to others and ask questions?

9. Do you make judgments slowly, weighing all the facts first?

10. Do you have plenty of *enthusiasm*?

The most interesting thing about these characteristics is that no one is born with them. They are all *acquired,* and that means that *you can have them too!* It's not possible to develop these traits or characteristics all at once; but once you go to work on them, you'll see that each one of the traits you develop makes the others that follow easier to acquire.

⟹ HOW YOU USE YOUR MIND WILL DECIDE WHAT YOU MAKE OF YOUR LIFE.

⟹ THE GREATEST POWER OF THE MIND IS *IMAGINATION*.

⟹ DAILY EXERCISES WILL DEVELOP AND STRENGTHEN THE IMAGINATION.

6

How to Become Popular

Have you ever watched someone you considered popular and wished that you could be just like them? Do you think that fate seems to bless some people with an intangible something that irresistibly draws others to them?

Just like success in any other aspect of your life, popularity is *not* a gift that is bestowed on some and not handed out to others. To become popular, *you have to work at it*. There are a number of habits that you must develop and a certain amount of effort that you have to expend if you want to be popular.

If you honestly work every day on developing the habits discussed on the following pages, you will gain recognition and respect within your school and community. It won't be long before your classmates and friends will be looking to *you* for *approval*. You'll have more dates, you will have more opportunities to do what you want to do, and your life will be much more enjoyable.

By the way, if you think that you don't "look good enough" to be popular, think again. The word *attractive* has little or nothing to do with your physical looks. It doesn't make one bit of difference what you look like on the outside! There are just as many physically beautiful people who are lonely and friendless as there are physically not-so-perfect people who are well liked, fun to be with, and admired.

Smile

I f you truly want to be popular, you must develop an outgoing personality, and that starts with a *smile*. From this minute on—and *for the rest of your life*—involve yourself in other people's lives by smiling at everyone with whom you come in contact! Meet another person's eyes with your own. Hold your head high (but don't stick your nose in the air!). Be sure when you say hello to someone that you *smile* when you say it. Use the other person's name if you know it. A person considers his or her own name the most important name in the world.

What if you don't feel like smiling? Do it anyway! It won't take long for your smile to become a habit—a delightful trademark—that special something people will remember about you.

Try this test: if you have a tape recorder, or can borrow one, turn it on to "record" and read the following sentence *without* a smile: "Hello, my name is ____. What's yours?"

Now put a big smile on your face; a warm, eye-sparkling smile, and repeat that sentence: "Hello, my name is _____ . What's yours?"

Now play back both sentences. Amazing, isn't it? Which of those greetings would you most like to hear from a stranger? The smiling one, of course!

If you don't have a tape recorder, ask someone in your family, or a friend, to stand with his or her back to you. Then say, "Hello, my name is _____. What's yours?'' without a smile. Now do it again, this time with your best smile. Ask whoever helped you if he or she noticed any difference between the two sentences.

Now you're ready for the mirror test. Stand in front of a mirror and repeat your two sentences just as you did before. Aren't you pleased with what you see when you smile?

Smiles don't have to be seen; they can be heard and felt. We've just proved that. From now on, never answer a phone without smiling as you pick up the receiver. You don't have to turn yourself into a clown. Just keep the corners of your mouth turned up!

And besides, there's a built-in bonus. It's a known scientific fact that it is much easier to feel good and be happy when you wear a smile. It's also been proved that a smile is beneficial for the muscles and the other tissues of your face. In fact, there are *no* disadvantages to a sincere smile!

So, when you wake up each day, put your best smile on before you put on your clothes. If you do, whatever you wear will look like a million dollars. (If you wear a frown, no matter what your clothes cost, you aren't going to look your best.)

Be interested in others

B eing friendly means being—or becoming—a friend. In order to do this, you have to be *interested* in other people, *not* just yourself. *Being interested in others will create more friendships for you than trying to make others interested in you.*

If you don't learn this lesson, it won't matter what else you do, because you will never be popular in the magical sense of that word. Look around you at the people you know. The ones who are the most enjoyable to be with and the ones who have the greatest number of friends are *genuinely* concerned about others. Those who are alone and unhappy are self-centered and interested mainly in themselves.

Think about the people you know. Which of them do you most enjoy being with? Are they the ones who are interested in what you have been doing and what you think? Doesn't it please you when a friend or relative remembers to ask you the outcome of something you had planned to do? It makes you feel important, doesn't it? This is another key to becoming popular. *Make your friends and acquaintances feel that they are important*.

One of the ways you can show interest is to listen carefully when someone talks to you. Don't interrupt them. You have so much to gain by getting into this habit. In addition to making the other person feel important, you can learn a lot! Encourage people to talk about themselves; listening and learning from others is an education that you can't afford to miss. When you pay courteous attention to others, *you* benefit!

Help others

Helping others can—if handled correctly—demonstrate that you are not a selfish person and that you are able to and like to share things with others. Don't, however, push your idea of help onto someone who obviously isn't interested. *Offer a sincere hand when you can see it is both needed and wanted*. For instance, if you are doing well in a particular area of activity and you can see that someone else in the same endeavor is having difficulty, find an opportunity to offer your help. (Never offer help in front of others if you think it could be embarrassing.) If classmates accept your help, you may want to find a way to let them reciprocate. This will put you on equal ground, and they won't feel that you're showing off or being superior. A good example of helpful behavior might go something like this:

In school, you get good grades in a language course, and the girl behind you—we'll call her Mary—is really having trouble with this week's assignment. Mary is also in a science class with you and getting better grades than you. When the class ends, you turn to her, smile, and say, "Mary, do you suppose we could get together and give each other a little help? I've been having a hard time with our science assignment. Would you like to study our language and science assignments together?"

In this diplomatic way, you have offered your help *and* made her feel important. You both benefit. Helping each other is what makes this world go around. We all need one another. *No one person has all the answers to all the questions* and nothing can ever make, you feel better than genuinely helping another person. You will earn gratitude and respect for your help. And these are the cornerstones of popularity.

Keep yourself looking good

That's basic. *Always* look your best. If you sincerely do this, you don't need a lot of money for expensive clothes or the latest fashions. The way you take care of yourself tells others what you think about yourself. *If you let yourself go, you won't respect yourself, and if you don't respect yourself, why should anyone else?*

Develop your values

Truly popular people are people with strong values— sometimes called moral codes or ethics. These are the basic beliefs by which a person lives. It is important for you to develop a high set of these values. Perhaps the easiest way to do this is to follow the Golden Rule— *never* do to another person what you would *not* want another person to do to you. Show the same respect for others' feelings that you want others to show you.

Another thing to remember is: when you are wrong, *admit it*. If you have unintentionally hurt someone's feelings, ask for forgiveness the moment you realize it. The hurt will heal much faster that way. And if someone admits a mistake to you, go out of your way to make them feel comfortable and at ease. It takes honesty and courage to acknowledge your errors and that kind of behavior should be encouraged!

Never, never betray a confidence. If a person tells you a secret, make sure it remains a secret. If a person talks to you as a friend and reveals information about personal matters and problems, make sure that these confidences go no further.

Be honest with yourself and it will be easier to be honest with others. Being honest with yourself means not kidding yourself about anything. If you don't lie to yourself, you won't lie to others. People will trust you and come to rely on you.

Be a leader, not a follower

S ometimes being a leader means being different. Being a leader means that you don't always follow the crowd. Just because "everyone" is doing something doesn't necessarily make it right, or even fun!

Don't let someone else make your decisions, especially if those decisions affect your set of values. Listen carefully when you hear that little voice inside you say,

"Should I?" Whenever you're in doubt, ask yourself if what you are thinking of doing would hurt someone else; would betray your values; or would cause you embarrassment if others found out. Cowards are *afraid* to say no. You aren't a coward! You have the courage and strength to be a leader.

You might be afraid that being this kind of a leader will hurt your popularity, but this isn't so; *it will increase it*. Just try it and see for yourself.

Be willing to change

D o you think that there are some things about yourself that might annoy people or put them off in some way? Sit down where you can have some privacy and take a blank piece of paper. Fold it in half lengthwise. In the upper left-hand corner, write the word *plus*. In the upper right-hand corner, write the word *minus*. Now you are ready to make a list of the things you *do* like about yourself and a list of things you *don't* like and might want to change.

For example, ask yourself the question: "Am I a fair person? Do I try to see both sides of a situation?" If the answer is yes, write "I am fair" on the plus side of your sheet.

Do people ever say: "Boy, are you impatient!" or "You are never on time!"? Do you make promises you know you can't keep? Write down these "deficiencies" on the minus side.

Do you do your best in school or at work? Do you fulfill your responsibilities at home? Think about these questions; then put your responses under the appropriate heading.

Don't try to complete this list in one sitting. Work on it for a while, and then put it away for a day or so.

Ask someone in your family or a close friend what they see as your greatest assets and what they see as your greatest liabilities. In a few days, you should have a fairly honest picture of yourself. Be sure to date your paper and put it in a safe place where you can take it out for another evaluation at a later time.

Now that you are thinking of ways in which to change, get yourself a notebook for a "daily review." Set aside an "alone time" at the end of each day—just before going to bed would be fine—and write down all the things you did in the course of the day in blocks of one-hour time frames. This will give you a picture that will help you see the things that you are proud of accomplishing and those things that weren't so great and that you might want to change or approach in a different way the next time around. Blocking out your time in one-hour intervals will also show you where you are wasting time. This "alone time" and the daily review will give you a chance to collect your thoughts and plan for the next day.

When you are fairly certain that you have been thorough in your self-analysis, both in your plus-minus list and your daily reviews, you'll begin to see areas you want to change. And guess what? Writing them down—*admitting them*—was the hard part! The rest will be easy. The only rule for making a change is that *you must sincerely want to change*. If you do, *you will*. It's that easy.

Be aware

Keep yourself informed of current events. Listen and watch the news on radio and TV; read the newspapers and one or more of the news magazines. You are a part of this world. It's important for you to be aware of what's happening in your local community, as well as around the globe. People who are in the know are automatically more interesting. This part of your development increases in importance as you get older. Don't ever limit your knowledge. Learning should be a life-long project. When you cease to learn, you cease to be.

Be involved

W e all have special interests. Develop yours. If you are in school, find out what extracurricular activities are available to you. Are you interested in student government, sports, dramatics, music, debate, civic projects, work-study programs?

Obviously, you can't join every group! Pick one or two that interest you most. Then, give those interests your very best efforts.

Even though you can't be a part of every social or interest group, you can *care* about the others. Don't limit your friends or relationships to a small circle, either. Go out of your way to learn about other groups and clubs. Meet people whose interests and backgrounds differ from yours. If you are in sports, take the time to go to the school or community plays and debates. Find out who your student government representatives are and talk to them. Find out what others are doing and how they became involved in their own interest groups. Not only will you make new friends, but you'll be learning through the person-to-person exchange.

Learn to cooperate

B ecome involved in efforts in which you work with others for the benefit of everyone. It isn't possible to achieve or do everything on your own. Work with the members of your class, your community, and your family to achieve something that you all want. Become involved in a project at school where the total effort of everyone is needed. Your efforts and talents can make a big difference.

Be enthusiastic

Whatever you do, *do it with enthusiasm!* Enthusiasm makes life—and you—exciting. Every act accomplished with enthusiasm is *more* successful, *more* rewarding.

Enthusiasm will improve your looks and your personality. *Enthusiasm* is contagious. It will attract others to you, fill your life with joy, and bring you rewards in school and in your job. It will motivate you and make you an achiever. *Enthusiasm* will make you a positive thinker. It will destroy fear and build character. With *enthusiasm* you will really be alive! *Enthusiasm* is the difference between being a winner and being a loser.

Enthusiasm is the art of putting everything you have to work for you in everything you do.

When you wake up each morning, think of the day as if it were the biggest day of your life! Remember that every person you meet and everything you do can have a profound effect on reaching your goal of becoming respected, well liked, and *popular.* Nothing will keep your enthusiasm more alive than continually remembering what it is that you want to achieve.

Walk through each day as though you have already become very popular. Whenever you are reaching for a goal, pretend *at all times* that you've actually reached it. This conscious positive attitude will build the characteristics that accompany your goal. It won't take long for you to see that you're no longer pretending to be someone popular and exciting. *You* are *someone popular and exciting!*

➤ KEEP A SMILE ON YOUR FACE.
➤ BE FRIENDLY.
➤ GIVE SINCERE HELP TO OTHERS.
➤ ALWAYS LOOK GOOD.
➤ DEVELOP HIGH VALUES.
➤ DON'T BE AFRAID TO BE DIFFERENT—BE A LEADER.
➤ WORK ON MAKING CHANGES IN YOUR LIFE.
➤ KEEP YOURSELF INFORMED.
➤ GET INVOLVED!
➤ SHOW YOUR ENTHUSIASM.

7

C.P.S.T.: The Answer to Your Problems

P
icture yourself lost in a desert. All you have with you are the clothes that you are wearing. The sun is beating down on you and you are exhausted and very thirsty.

In the distance you can see a house that looks like a castle. Because you've been in the desert for so long, you wonder if it isn't a mirage—it seems too good to be true. But even though the castle might just be there in your imagination, you can't take the chance of not heading toward it. You know that you will die if you don't get out of the heat and quench your thirst.

You begin to walk toward the building, hoping that it will be real. The closer you get, the more beautiful the building becomes. It's made of stone, so you reason that it has to be cooler inside. Much cooler! You are nearly there. Your throat is aching. Because of the heat, it is nearly swollen shut. If it weren't for the castle in front of you, you would be tempted to lie down in the sand and give up.

You are close enough now to see that the castle isn't a mirage. It's real! Through the open door, you can see a beautiful fountain in the entryway. You can actually smell the cool, fragrant water. All you have to do is walk a few more feet and you'll be at the door, which is already standing open as if to welcome you.

All of a sudden, the wind comes up and just as you are about to reach the doorway, a gust of air blows the door shut. You reach for the handle and find that it is locked!

If that had really happened to you, what would you do? Would you give the door a good kick, then turn and walk away?

Hardly! If your life depended on it, you would find a way to get inside that castle! You would probably walk around looking for a window low enough to climb through, or perhaps another door that isn't locked. You might have to walk around a couple of times before you figured out exactly how to do it, but you would find a way, wouldn't you?

Not all problems in your life will be a matter of life or death, but you will *have plenty of them.* That's for sure! Everybody does.

How do you view your problems?

Do you look at problems as though they were placed before you to irritate you or to slow you down? Do you think that the problems in your life were specifically designed to stop you from getting the things that you want?

If you are a person with a negative attitude, you look at problems as stop signs or barricades. To a negative person, a problem is a convenient cop-out.

If you're a person with a positive attitude, you know that *problems are nothing more than healthy chal-*

lenges. They appear in your life to give you strength, by testing your courage, intelligence, and determination.

Another way to consider your problems is to look at them as though they were hurdles in a race at a track meet. Training begins with low hurdles. You practice and practice until you can clear the low ones. When you can easily clear these, you move on to practice on a higher set.

It's important for you to solve all the problems that you find in front of you now. As you do, you're building your mental mucles so that if and when your problems become more complex, you will still be able to solve them without their getting in the way of the rest of the things in your life.

Learning to solve problems can be an exciting way to test your creativity! Sometimes—like the problem of how to get inside the castle—the answer is obvious. To solve that particular one, you have to find or make another entrance. The solutions to your own actual problems, however, may not always be so obvious.

When you come up against a problem for which the solution is not immediately apparent, it's time to start using the six steps of C.P.S.T.—*Creative Problem Solving Technique.*

Step #1: Put your problem down on paper

First, you must write down the problem in its simplest form. That might take some effort, because we generally think of our problems as being complicated. Begin by fully explaining your problem on paper. Put in all the facts as you understand them. Here's an example:

I've lost the textbook that I need for English class. I've looked all over for it and it's nowhere to be found. I have checked with the school library and they don't have an extra copy for me to borrow. I need the book to complete my semester assignment. In order to replace the book, I will need $15—which I don't have. I don't want to ask Mom or Dad for the money, because they have yelled at me about the way I carelessly mislay my personal belongings.

I have an opportunity to go to a nearby city with my best friend's family this weekend. They offered to pay for my motel room and meals, but I have to bring my own spending money. My friend is taking $25. I'd like to go, but I don't have the money. I know that it wouldn't be much fun if I couldn't go shopping with my friend or do any sightseeing for which there might be a charge.

For Christmas, I gave my brother a beautifully wrapped box with a note in it entitling him to be taken to see his favorite horror movie when it came to town during the year. Unfortunately, it came to town this week, and I am broke.

Take a look at what you've written. You have a lot of problems! Or have you? It looks like you really have only one problem. When you reduce everything you have written to its simplest terms, your problem is *lack of money.* In other words, if you had some money, none of the items that you listed would be a problem!

Step #2: Brainstorm

B rainstorming can be done by one person or a group of people but all of you must have a positive attitude. To begin this process, take a sheet of paper and write your *simply stated definition of your problem* at the top of the page. Then comes the creative and fun part! *Thinking positively,* list as many possible ways of obtaining that money as you are able. Don't worry about how practical they are! Don't try to put them in any order. Don't worry about whether or not they are far out! Just write—as fast as you can—and list as many as you can think of.

This step of C.P.S.T. is concerned with quantity, not quality. Most of the time we are urged to stress *quality* over *quantity.* This time it's different. The more options you can list the better! This project will help you exercise your creativity and let you enjoy your own cleverness!

Your list might look something like this:

Borrow from mother.
Borrow from father.
Win lottery.
Sell bicycle I never use.
Sell old skis.
Organize a car wash with friends and split profits.
Go to senior citizen's complex and offer to do grocery shopping for 10 percent of total grocery bill.
Go door to door and offer to wash windows, rake leaves, mow lawns, shovel snow, run errands.
Collect old paperback books from anyone who will donate them and have a second-hand book sale.
Ask neighbors if they would like to have a garage sale if I agree to do all the work. (You would take a percentage of everything that you sell for them.)

Run an ad in paper telling my age and listing my experience, asking for an opportunity to do odd jobs at $＿＿＿＿ per hour.

Baby-sit.

Call newspaper and see if they need any substitute carriers for anyone who is ill or on vacation.

Read help wanted ads in newspaper every evening.

Go from door to door in the business district and ask store managers if they need any temporary help or if they have any short-term projects that I could do.

Organize a group of friends and have a bake sale. (Be sure to check and see if your city or town requires you to obtain a permit for this kind of sale.)

Step #3: Seek advice from others

If you aren't confident that your list will produce the solution to your problem, make another list! This second list should have the names of everyone that you can think of who might be able to give you advice. Telephone or visit those people. Explain to them that you have a problem. Tell them that you respect their opinions and ask them if they would be willing to give you some suggestions on how to work through your dilemma.

Don't ever be afraid, ashamed, or embarrassed to ask for help from someone else, no matter how creative you become or how old you are. By the same token, don't depend on other people to solve your problems for you. The people to whom you turn for help are just that—*helpers*. It's up to *you* to find the solution that best answers your own needs. Take the suggestions of those people to whom you have gone for advice and add them to your list.

Step #4: Look for combinations of ideas

T ake another look at the list in the example. There are several ideas that can be combined in it that might help you reach a solution.

> I could run an ad in the paper or on the local radio station and sell both my bike *and* my skis.

> I could go to the senior citizen's complex and offer to run errands for them or do odd jobs in their buildings. These same people might have paperback books they would be willing to contribute to my second-hand sale, or they might be interested in buying books from this sale. Maybe I could take the books from door to door in a wagon!

> If I decide to have a cooperative garage sale, I could sell my bike and my skis there.

Step #5: Look for ways to expand any of your ideas

S tudy the example again and you'll realize these options are possible if time allows.

> I might decide to have a *strictly teen* garage

sale and advertise it on the bulletin board at school.

Instead of doing regular baby-sitting, I could get a couple of my friends and put together a baby-sitting center in my home on Friday and Saturday. (This would be a fantastic idea if you lived in a large neighborhood or subdivision. Parents could drop off their children and pick them up at your home. Instead of making $5 or $6 for an evening of baby-sitting, you could make $30 or more by doing it this way. To let people know that your service is available, make up some fliers enthusiastically outlining the creative ideas you have for caring for and entertaining children.)

Step #6: Check your list and see if you might simplify an idea

In our example, there is at least one place where an idea can be made easier and therefore more workable.

Instead of organizing a group of friends to work together on a bake sale, I could go door to door in my neighborhood and let people know that I am trying to raise some money for a personal project and that I am taking orders for chocolate chip cookies (or whatever you bake best), which I will make and deliver for $_____ per dozen.

Once you have completed the six steps in the C.P.S.T., you will see that there isn't any problem that you can't find a solution for this way! Just remember that no matter how serious or how simple your problem, you don't need to panic. With your *creativity, positive attitude,* and *enthusiasm*—along with *C.P.S.T.*—you have everything you need to solve any problem!

⟶ EVERYBODY HAS PLENTY OF PROBLEMS.
⟶ PROBLEMS ARE NOTHING MORE THAN *HEALTHY CHALLENGES.*
⟶ LEARNING TO SOLVE YOUR PROBLEMS WILL DEVELOP YOUR CREATIVITY.
⟶ THE SIX-STEP C.P.S.T. WILL HELP YOU SOLVE ANY PROBLEM.

8

The Easy Way to Find and Keep a Job

I n the chapter on goals, we talk about your future career or life's work and how to start planning for it now so you can be sure of earning an income in an industry or profession that you will enjoy. Before you reach that stage in your life, however, you will probably need to find a job to help move you toward a goal—a job to help pay your tuition or expenses in school; a part-time job to provide you with spending money; a summer job; a job to help you buy your first car. For whatever reason you need the job, *the principles of getting and keeping any job are the same:*

- Have a positive attitude.
- Be willing to do more than just what is necessary.
- Give a little before you expect to receive.

Sixteen-year-old Terri was looking for a job. Her parents had told her that she could have a car if she bought it herself. Terri was excited. She would have her own wheels and not have to depend on her parents to drive her where she wanted to go.

There was an ad in the newspaper for part-time help wanted at a local bookstore. Terri was more than a little interested because her favorite pastime was reading, and she figured that working in a bookstore would be a great job for her. The ad stated that the manager would be taking applications for the position on the following Tuesday, between 4:00 and 5:30 in the afternoon.

On Tuesday, when Terri arrived at the store, she was disappointed to see how many other people were there ahead of her. There were six of them, all filling out applications. Some of the applicants were older and Terri presumed that they had had experience in other jobs. Instead of filling out the application, Terri left the store. On the way home, she ran into Ted, a friend from school.

Terri told Ted about wanting to find a job so that she could buy a car. She explained that she had planned to apply for the job at the bookstore but had decided against it when she saw how many other people had the same idea. "I was the youngest person there. I'm sure the manager would hire someone with experience before he would hire me," she told Ted.

Ted told Terri about a plan that he had used once when he wanted a job where there were other applicants. He told her to go back and get the application and fill it out. "On the line at the bottom where it says 'Remarks,' just write that you understand that there are others who want the job, but ask the boss to talk to you before he hires anyone for the position. Tell him that you can *prove* that you are the best qualified if you are given the chance to speak to him personally. When you get the interview, call me and I'll tell you what to do next."

Ted was very convincing, so Terri turned around and went back to the store and filled out an application. She wrote what Ted had told her to write at the bottom of the page.

Two days later, Terri received a call from Mr. Waltham, the manager of the store. "What did you mean by your remarks at the bottom of the application?" he asked her.

"Sir, may I come and explain?" she asked.

"I suppose it won't hurt for me to listen. Can you be here tomorrow afternoon around four o'clock?"

"Of course. I'll be there by four. And thank you for the opportunity to talk with you," Terri concluded.

Terri called Ted and told him about the interview. "What's the next step?" she wanted to know.

They talked for fifteen minutes and when they hung up, Terri thought to herself, *This is going to work. I have a feeling that I'm really going to get that job!*

Terri arrived at the bookstore just before 4:00 and waited until the manager was free to talk with her. He asked her again what made her think that he should hire her—someone with no experience—over a more mature person who had previous job experience.

With a confident smile, Terri looked the manager in the eye and said, "I need this job, Mr. Waltham. I'm honest and I'm a hard worker. I'll prove that I'm good with people and that I can take orders if you will allow me to work for you with no pay for one week. At the end of that time, if you are satisfied that I can do the job, perhaps you will hire me. If I prove that I'm not the right person for you, I'll leave and you will have had my help for free."

"Well," said Mr. Waltham, "that's certainly one I haven't heard before! You must really want the job, Terri. What have I got to lose?"

The two looked at each other and Mr. Waltham smiled. "I'll give you your chance. Be here at three o'clock tomorrow afternoon. For the next week, you'll be working from three until eight. At the end of the week, we'll talk again.''

Terri looked around the store before she left and whispered to herself as she walked through the door, ''Mr. Waltham, you don't know it yet; but I'm going to be the best part-time help you've ever had!''

Terri met Ted in the hall at school the next morning. ''It worked! He's giving me a chance! Thanks, Ted. You really knew what you were talking about. Got any other advice?''

''Well, as long as you're asking! What time are you supposed to start working?''

Terri explained the hours and conditions. Ted said, ''Instead of arriving right at three, make sure that you are there and ready to work at least ten minutes early. If there's ever a time when you have finished what Waltham's asked you to do and he doesn't suggest that you start something else, *find* something to do! Even if it's dusting the books or sweeping the floor. Keep busy. Let him see that you don't have to be watched all the time. Let him know that you can be depended on to do whatever needs doing. When it's time to quit, don't immediately stop what you are doing. Finish whatever it is that you're working on. Oh, there's one other thing. Whenever you don't quite understand how to do things properly, make sure you ask. You want to be sure that you're doing things the way he wants them done.''

Terri followed Ted's advice to the letter. At the end of the week, Mr. Waltham asked her how she liked her work.

''I love it!'' said Terri enthusiastically. ''I hope that you are going to decide to let me stay.''

''Terri, you did just what you said you were going to do. You've proved that you're a good, honest worker. I like the way you keep busy and are always on time. Except for the time that my wife worked here, I never had an employee who wasn't anxious to leave when it was quitting time. The job's yours; and I'm mighty glad to have you.''

How to look for a job

B efore actually looking for a job, make a list of the skills you have to offer (use the brainstorming technique discussed in the C.P.S.T. chapter to help with the list). If you are still in high school, your skills may be limited, but this shouldn't stop you. There are many nontechnical or nonspecific skilled positions, such as waiting tables, selling in retail stores, typing, helping out in dry cleaners or coffee shops, or taking on a delivery route. The opportunities are endless.

After you have an idea of what you can offer, begin to look in your community for a business that might be able to use your skills.

• Check the classified section of your local newspaper under the help wanted column.

• Ask your friends who have jobs to let you know if they hear of any openings where they work.

• Check and see if there are any employment agencies in your community who place people of your age and skills.

• Take the yellow pages of your phone book and go up and down the pages, listing the companies you feel might need your services.

• You may know of a company for whom you would really like to work. Go in person and ask if they are currently hiring. If they say no, ask to fill out an application anyway. Tell them how much you admire their company and how much you would like to work for them and that you will check back periodically. Make a note on your calendar to call those people every two weeks. If you are determined to get a job with the company, it may take time, but eventually you will!

If you really want a job, knock on as many doors as you can find! Make the best impression you can. *Be confident.* Let employers know that you are *anxious* to work. Let them know that you are honest and that you are willing to prove to them that *you* are a good investment for them by investing your *own* time without anything but the promise of a chance.

Once you have a job...

P ractice the following principles to show your employer that you are the best person for the job.

1. Get there early and get right to work. A job is where you go to work, not where you go to socialize.

2. If there is something you don't understand, don't hesitate to ask questions.

3. If you complete a task, and your supervisor isn't right there to tell you what to start next, *use your initiative* and start something on your own.

4. Use your creativity; *look* for an opportunity to do more than you have been asked to do; *look* for better ways to do what you are already doing.

5. When it's quitting time, *finish* the project you are working on. Don't just drop everything and head for the door.

6. Do your job as though it were the most important thing you've ever done. Don't be satisfied with being good at your job. *Be the best.*

7. Be loyal to your job and your employer. Never say anything about either unless it is positive.

8. Be enthusiastic about your work and friendly to

the people you meet on the job.

9. Remember, if you do *only* what you are told, you can't expect a raise or a promotion If you do *more* than you are told, you can be *sure* of a raise or promotion.

10. Do your job as though you were the boss. Eventually you will be!

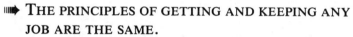

IID➤ THE PRINCIPLES OF GETTING AND KEEPING ANY JOB ARE THE SAME.

IID➤ HAVE A POSITIVE ATTITUDE, AND GIVE BEFORE YOU EXPECT TO RECEIVE.

IID➤ KNOCK ON AS MANY DOORS AS YOU CAN!

IID➤ IF YOU WANT A RAISE OR A PROMOTION, DO *MORE* THAN IS EXPECTED OF YOU, BE LOYAL TO YOUR EMPLOYER AND DO YOUR JOB AS THOUGH IT IS THE MOST IMPORTANT THING YOU'VE EVER DONE.

IID➤ DO YOUR JOB AS THOUGH YOU WERE THE BOSS!

9

You Always Have a Choice

H ave you ever wondered who decides who will be successful; who will reach their goals; who will have the things they want the most? Do you think it's the same person who decides who will live uneventful, boring lives and who will never have the material things that can make them happy? The answer to those questions is *each one of us is responsible for the person we become and for the things we have*.

If *you* become the person you want to be, or acquire the things you want most, it is because *you did something*. If *you* live day to day without doing anything to be proud of and never acquire the things that will make you happy, it's because you made the choice *not* to do whatever was necessary. *The choice is always yours*.

When you pick out a blouse or shirt in the morning, change the station on your radio, ask someone to have lunch with you, or make plans to see a movie, these are all choices.

Every day brings more and more opportunities for choices or decisions. These choices won't always be easy to make. There will be plenty of times in your life where the choices are difficult, and the decisions pain-

ful. You may find yourself very confused. The best way
to test a choice is to ask yourself two important questions: *Am I making this choice, or is someone else
making it for me? Is this choice right for me, or is it
right for someone else?*

Sarah is fourteen years old. I met her in the Detroit
airport. She had been sitting across from me in the
waiting area with her head down, staring at her shoes,
for about a half hour. She looked so sad, I just wanted
to do something that would make her smile. I bought a
couple of candy bars and asked her if she would like
one.

Sarah shook her head no. I waited a few minutes
and asked her if she was heading home or going on a
vacation. She just shifted uneasily in her seat and said,
"I don't know."

This seemed like such a strange answer to me that
I couldn't resist asking, "You don't know where you're
going?"

"I'm going to my father's house. My mother lives
here in Detroit. I don't know where 'home' is. One of
them gets me for six months, the other one gets me for
the other six."

I waited a few minutes and then introduced myself.
I told her that I really hated traveling alone and asked
her if she would mind sitting with me, since we were
boarding the same airplane for Florida. Sarah just
shrugged. I took that to mean that she would be delighted
to have my company. (I had made up my mind that she
was going to smile before we left one another!)

We made small talk for a long time, and later when
we were in the air and had finished our meal, I asked
Sarah why she seemed so unhappy.

"I don't have any choices," she said. "Everything

that happens to me is planned by somebody else. My mother, my father, my friend Lucy, and my teachers. I might as well be a robot!''

"Which one of them decided how you should feel about your trip today?'' I asked.

"What do you mean?''

"Well, you seem to feel pretty bad about having to leave Detroit. Who decided that you should feel that way?''

Sarah looked at me as if I had two heads and said, "That's a dumb question. I feel bad because I *feel bad*. I don't want to leave now. There was a dance next week that I wanted to go to. A dumb old dance.''

"Terrific! Sarah, you made the choice yourself. You aren't a robot, you're a person! I'm really glad to know that, because I don't have much experience talking to robots!'' For a minute, I thought that Sarah was going to get up and move because she was looking at me like I was a little strange.

"What do you mean, I made a choice?''

"Well, you said that you feel bad because *you feel bad,* not because someone else feels bad or because someone told you to feel bad. You made the choice to feel bad—and you do! That shows me that you made at least one choice on your own today.''

Sarah just stared straight ahead for a couple of minutes. Finally, she looked at me and said, "You don't make any sense. Choice means you can pick from more than one thing. I can't see that I had more than one thing to pick from, can you?''

"Sarah, I don't know you well enough to know what all your choices were, but I can see that you had at least two others besides the one you finally chose. First, you could have explained how much the dance meant to you, and then asked your father and your mother if it would have been possible to postpone your trip to Florida for one more week.

"Another choice would have been to be happy about your trip to your father's home. You could have looked at it as an adventure! You never know what's going to happen before it happens! Who knows, you might be in for the most exciting six months of your life during your time at your father's! Do you see what I mean? By feeling sorry for yourself and keeping your eyes focused on the floor or on your shoes, you're missing a lot of things that are going on around you. There isn't much of a chance that anything pleasant or happy will happen when you're in this frame of mind."

Sarah and I talked nonstop about choices and consequences for the rest of the trip. We decided that *the choices you face in your life right now are important. It's what you do about these choices today that will shape your future.*

When you sit around and do nothing, *you are making a choice;* you are choosing *not* to do something. You have to pay the consequences. If *you* choose to complain about every single thing that happens to you every day, then *you* have to accept the fact that not many people are going to want to share your company. (It's too depressing to be around a constant complainer!)

If *you* choose to do all your assignments in school to the best of your ability, then *you* will have to accept the pride of accomplishment and the honors that come with it.

If *you* choose to watch what you eat and take care of yourself, then *you* will have to accept a nice, healthy-looking body that does what you want it to do (and gets complimentary looks from others!).

If *you* choose to keep a smile on your face no matter how you feel, and be optimistic that things will work out for the best, then *you* will have to accept the fact that your phone will be busy all the time and you'll have lots of friends.

The plane landed and Sarah and I headed for the gate together. She pointed out her father to me as soon as she saw him. Before we reached the spot where he was standing, we said our good-byes. Sarah ran up to her father and gave him a hug and a kiss, and she was smiling one of the happiest smiles I've ever seen! As I passed by them, I heard her father say, "Sarah, I'd forgotten how really beautiful you are! I'm so glad you're here!"

If Sarah *kept* smiling and *chose* to be happy that she was with her father, what kind of a visit do you think she had?

Choices. Choices. Choices.

Tom, a twenty-six-year-old man living in Indiana, has a partnership in a prosperous business because of a choice he made when he was fifteen years old.

Tom was the third oldest child in a family of seven. One of his younger brothers, Johnny, was chronically ill, and it took all the money that his parents could earn to pay Johnny's medical bills. Both parents worked, and when they were at home they spent a lot of time with Johnny. There wasn't much time left over for all the other things that parents usually do.

Tom had a lot of friends. None of these friends were rich, but they did live in nice homes. Tom could remember how his home had looked when his parents had had time to take care of it—before Johnny came along and then got sick. Tom hated to have his friends over because the place really looked shabby now.

Tom kept the grass cut, but there were no longer

any flowers in the yard and the bushes hadn't been trimmed in so long that they were spindly and ugly.

The house next door had just been bought by two elderly ladies, and when Tom came home from school one day, he saw them out in their yard planting flowers and pulling weeds. This went on for several weeks, and it wasn't long before the ladies' yard began to look beautiful. In fact, the whole house next door looked different. Flowers had started poking their heads up and the colors were perky and cheerful.

Tom stopped to talk to the ladies one afternoon and he told them that he thought they had done a great job with their new place. The ladies said that they thought Tom was "a nice chap" for taking the time to pay them a compliment. As he was leaving, Tom said, "I sure wish our yard looked as nice as yours."

"It could, if you wanted it to," said one of the ladies.

"You don't understand. We're kinda poor because of my little brother. He's sick and we have to take him to the doctor a lot. Mom and Dad don't have any money to do things with. That's why our place looks so bad."

"Young man," said the other lady, "since when is it your parents' job to see that your house looks nice? It's your home, too, isn't it?"

Tom was beginning to feel uncomfortable and his face began to flush. "Yes, ma'am. I live here too."

"Well, what are you waiting for? Get yourself a bucket and some soapy water and wash off that front porch and the door. When you finish that come back over and we'll give you some plants and a couple of packages of flower seeds. There's no reason why you can't make your own place look as good as ours!"

Tom found an empty bucket, filled it with water, and went out to see what he could do about the porch.

He was surprised to see how much better it looked when he finished!

As promised, the two ladies offered him some of their extra plants and seeds. Before accepting the ladies' gifts, Tom looked over toward his house and asked his new friends if they were sure anything besides weeds would grow there. The lawn had been neglected for a long time, and the earth looked dry and crumbly. The ladies agreed that it looked pretty bad, but suggested that he take a sample of the soil to the garden shop where they had bought their seeds and ask to have the earth examined.

On his way home from school the next day, Tom did as the ladies had suggested.

After checking the soil, the salesperson told Tom that the ground needed several different fertilizers. As it was now, it wasn't rich enough to grow anything.

That takes care of that, thought Tom. *I can't afford to buy anything and Dad never has any extra money.* Tom turned and left the shop. On his way home he became angry. *It just isn't fair!* he thought. *I'm tired of living in the worst-looking place on the street!*

Without really thinking about it, Tom turned around and headed back to the store. While he was angry, he had made a choice. He had decided *not* to live in the worst-looking house on the block.

He marched back into the store and asked the salesperson how much it would cost to buy the things he would need. The man figured everything out and handed Tom the list. Tom then asked if he could speak to the owner.

A man looked up from behind the counter, introduced himself as Mr. Davis, and then asked, "What can I do for you, son?"

"I was wondering if you would let me work for

you in return for the items here on this list."

Mr. Davis scratched his head and thought for a few minutes. "How old are you?" he asked.

"Fifteen," Tom answered.

"You're in school, aren't you?"

"Yes, but I could be here by three-thirty on week-days, or I could work for a while on Saturday," said Tom.

Mr. Davis didn't say anything and Tom continued. "It's like this," he said, lowering his voice. "I can't afford to pay for these things and our place looks real bad. My folks don't have any extra money and I have a couple of friends who said they'd show me how to fix up the yard."

"Well," said Mr. Davis, "I need someone to unload a truck tomorrow afternoon. Can you come by after school?"

"Yes, sir!"

Tom went to the shop the next day and for several days after that until he had put in enough hours to pay for the fertilizer and other items on his list.

With the help of his neighbors, Tom fertilized his yard, and planted the seeds and some small plants. In a few weeks, the yard began to show real signs of life!

When he walked up the sidewalk to his porch and saw how much better the grass looked and how much life the flowers added to the picture, he realized that the way the yard looked accounted for only about half of his pleasure. The biggest reward was the way he felt about having done it himself!

Mr. Davis began to call Tom regularly when he needed an extra pair of hands for a couple of hours, and Tom was paid part of the time. Other times he would work in exchange for a shrub or some kind of a plant. In addition to working for Mr. Davis, he was learning from him, too. Tom asked a lot of questions. He was discovering that he was quite interested in landscaping and plant care.

By the following summer, Tom's house had the best-looking yard on the street, and he had a job working for Mr. Davis after school, on Saturdays, and full-time in the summer.

By the time he graduated from high school, Tom definitely knew that he wanted to keep working at the garden shop. Mr. Davis advised him to think about going to college.

Things hadn't changed much for his parents in the money department, so Tom decided that he would live at home and commute to a college about forty miles away and be a part-time student. That way he could keep his job and earn enough to help out at home and pay his tuition.

He did very well in school and put what he learned to work for himself and Mr. Davis at the shop. Mr. Davis told one of his friends the year before Tom graduated that he was the best employee he had ever had. "He's more than an employee!" Mr. Davis said. "He's like a son. He cares as much about this business as I do. I don't mind saying that Tom has helped to build this business and make it a lot better than it was before."

Tom graduated from college when he was twenty-four years old, and as a graduation present, Mr. Davis gave him 15 percent of the business and offered him a chance to buy the remaining 85 percent at the time that Mr. Davis reached his sixty-fifth birthday.

Choices. They're sometimes kind of funny. A seemingly small choice like deciding to do something about the way a yard looked changed Tom's life.

Are the choices you make the right ones for you?

E d's father was a dentist. Ed's father's father had been a dentist. And guess what? Ed's great-grand-father had been a dentist! To make matters worse, they had all been named Edward. And they had all practiced in the same small community. Some of young Ed's friends teased him by saying that it was his great-great-great-grandfather who had made George Washington's teeth. It was a foregone conclusion that Ed would go to college and then on to dental school. After all, it was tradition!

Young Ed never thought about his future. He just did what his parents and relatives expected him to do. He graduated from high school and followed in the foot-steps of all the other Eds who had gone before him.

In his last year of dental school, Ed developed recurring headaches. It seemed as if his head was just one dull thud of pain all the time. He went from one doctor to another and no one could find the cause of his discomfort. In desperation, it was suggested that Ed see a psychologist and find out if perhaps the pain in his head was a symptom of his feelings rather than a medical problem.

Ed went to see a therapist named Dr. Markum. After the first couple of sessions, Dr. Markum was convinced that Ed's headaches were the result of the pressure that his family had been putting on him. Right after a particularly difficult test in school, Ed had an appointment with Dr. Markum. Holding his head in his hands, Ed suddenly blurted out: "I hate what I'm doing.

I don't want to be a dentist! I never did! All I really want to do is work with numbers. Too bad the men in my family weren't accountants. *That's* what I'd be better at.''

"Why don't you drop out of dental school and get your degree in accounting?'' the therapist asked simply.

"Are you crazy! My family would *die* if I didn't become a dentist! They've always said that it would be a disgrace to have a generation without a Dr. Ed. Besides, I can't change my mind now! I'm going to graduate in three weeks. Within a month, I'll be sharing an office with my father just like he shared an office with his father when he was my age. There's no way any of that can be changed now. It's just too late.''

"Ed, listen to yourself," said Dr. Markum. "Whose life are we talking about? You're twenty-six years old. You've been legally of age for years. You *own* your own life. It's not up to someone else to make your decisions. Think about it.''

Think about it. That's just about all Ed did for the next week. He thought and thought. He thought about how much it would hurt his father if he decided to change his plans. And it would probably kill his grandfather. What was he going to do? He telephoned his parents and told them that he wanted to come home for the weekend to talk about something important.

Because he was so close to graduating and had been dating a young woman named Vicky steadily for the past two years, his parents assumed that he was coming home to tell them that he was planning on getting married. They were thrilled, because Vicky would make a perfect wife for their son, and because all the other Eds had waited to get married until after they had graduated. More tradition.

Ed's news, needless to say, was a shock. After

taking Dr. Markum's advice, Ed had thought his situation through completely. This would be the end of the line. The tradition would have to break with him.

His father exploded. "What do you mean, you aren't going to finish dental school! You sure are! There's been a dentist in our family for more than a hundred years. You aren't going to end the tradition at this point!" Ed's father's face flushed a bright red and he shook his fist in the air. "We've given you everything, boy! You've had the best schools, best clothes, we've paid for your car, taken you on a great vacation every year! What do you mean you aren't going to become a dentist!"

"Just what I said, Dad," Ed replied quietly. "All my life you've made all my decisions for me. I've never done a thing on my own! Even my car! I wouldn't have minded paying for it myself—at least that way I could have had the one *I* wanted!"

"Ed, you're tired." His father's voice had taken on a condescending tone. "Graduation is just a couple of weeks away and you're under a lot of pressure. Why don't you forget about school for the weekend and relax. We can play golf tomorrow; you can see some of your friends, and when you go back on Sunday night you'll feel like a new person."

"Why won't you listen to what I'm saying!" Ed could see he was going to have to make his point more strongly. "I'm not going back. I've already had a meeting with the dean and told him about my decision. I've moved out of the apartment and I plan on getting a job so that I can earn my tuition for next semester at a different school. I'm going to get my degree in accounting. It's the thing I've always been best at. I don't understand why you want me to do something I hate when I can do something that I *want* to do."

The conversation went on for a while longer, but

Ed didn't back down. Dr. Markum had done his job well. He had shown Ed one of the things that can happen to a person who never makes a decision or a choice for himself.

It's great to do things that please other people; it's one of life's chief sources of pleasure and happiness—*but not when the thing that you are doing to please someone else doesn't please you as well.*

Consider all your options. Get as much *good* help and advice as you can. Make you *own* choices based on what will be best for *you* in the long run.

If you're in school, are you happy with the grades you're getting? Whatever your grades are, they are the ones that *you* have chosen to earn.

If you have a job, is it one that *you* enjoy? The way you feel about your job is *your* choice. The way you do your job is also *your* choice.

Do you get along well with other people? If you have only one friend or perhaps no friends, that's *your* choice. If you have a lot of friends and people respect you, it's because *you* made the choice to be the kind of person who is liked and respected.

Do you like the way your house looks? If you are living with your family, your parents have probably made the choice of where you live, but the way it looks is just as much *your choice* as theirs. What *is* your choice?

Do you want to earn $8,000 a year for the rest of your life, or would you like to make $100,000 or more a year? Who do you think will make the choice about your earning capacity?

The way you dress; the image you present; the way you speak; the way you walk; the friends you have; the degree of popularity you attain; the education you acquire; your future career. *All* these things are *your choices*, not someone else's. The way you spend your time, the places you visit, the house you will one day rent or buy—these are *your choices*.

What do you want out of today? What do you want out of this year? What do you want out of the rest of your life? When you do make your own choices, you are no longer a passenger in life; you are the driver. When you are the driver, the destination is up to you.

- ➠ YOU ARE THE ONLY ONE RESPONSIBLE FOR THE PERSON YOU BECOME AND THE THINGS YOU OWN.
- ➠ TO *BE* OR TO *HAVE* SOMETHING, YOU MUST *DO* SOMETHING.
- ➠ MAKE CHOICES THAT ARE *RIGHT FOR YOU*.
- ➠ WEIGH ALL THE FACTS, THEN MAKE A DECISION ON YOUR OWN.
- ➠ THE CHOICES YOU MAKE TODAY WILL SHAPE YOUR FUTURE.

10

Setting Goals

If you could have anything in the world that you want, what would it be? If you could become anything you desire, what would you become?

Everyone dreams. We all wish for the things we think would make us happy. You have, haven't you? Did you know that there is only *one* thing that stands between you and your dreams? That one thing is *work*.

There are millions and millions of people alive today who won't ever have what they want out of life because they only *wish* for their dreams. A wish is lazy. It says, "*Give* me something "

When a person ꞇtops wishing for something and starts to really *desire* it, that's different. Desire says, "I will work for what I want!" When *desire* gives your dream a push, you have a *goal*. Once that happens, you can make your dream come true.

You've seen what happens when the dreams of ordinary people become their goals. You see evidence of goals all around you. Those goals were just dreams at one time. They became reality through *desire*.

Everyone knows that Henry Ford invented the first assembly line automobile, but do you know the story behind that invention? It's the story of a young, very ordinary boy who used to daydream.

Henry Ford was born on a farm in Michigan. His

father wanted him to become a farmer just like himself. Henry didn't like the idea, because he really didn't love the land and animals the way his father did. *But,* whenever young Henry was given a job to do around the farm that sent him to the tool shed, that was something else. He loved repairing equipment and spent all his spare time thinking of ways to make farm work easier. His father often accused him of being lazy.

Henry's hobby was taking apart and putting back together anything that had moving parts. The year that he was twelve, his father gave him a watch for his birthday. Almost before he had even said "Thanks, Dad," he had the back off the watch and was carefully removing the parts. His father, outraged, said: "Do you have any idea how expensive that thing is, boy?!" Henry tried to explain that he just wanted to see how it worked in case it ever broke; that way he would be able to fix it. Mr. Ford had a very hard time understanding his son.

When Henry was thirteen, his mother died. He knew that he was going to have to be more help to his father, so he buckled down and tried to learn more about the business of farming. He avoided unnecessary trips to the tool shed until after his chores were done,

On a rare trip into town, Henry saw a steam-powered "horseless carriage" moving along the road. This was the first one he'd ever seen. He was speechless from excitement. A machine was moving under its own power! It was all Henry could think of for days. Seeing that engine turned his daydreams into *desire*. He wanted to make life easier for people and he was sure that the way to do it was through mechanical inventions.

It took many years. There were a lot of small successes along the way as well as some good-sized failures, but Henry kept plugging away. He wouldn't allow anything to keep him from working on his dream.

No matter where he worked or where he lived, a part of every day was devoted to pursuing his goal. Finally, the dream became a reality! Henry wasn't surprised. He'd been working for it all his life. He knew it would happen.

The Model T Ford automobile—made inexpensively on an assembly line—was the result of Henry's dream. That car changed history. It was a piece of machinery that the common man could afford. It set off a chain reaction around the world. Look at the way one *ordinary* man's dream altered the life of nearly everyone on earth!

Learning to set and work for short-term goals now will condition you for all the major goals you set during the rest of your life

G oals aren't just for the big things in your life, like the choice of a job or career, school, or how much money you want to earn. Goals are also for the less complicated and fun things you want out of life.

Climbing a flight of stairs is one way you can look at working toward a goal. Whether it's a short-term goal for today (a flight of three steps); an intermediate goal for this year (a flight of fourteen steps); or a lifetime pursuit (a flight of fifty steps), you progress the same way: it's always *one step at a time*.

From where you start—at the bottom—to the top,

where you reach your goal, may *look* like an impossible distance. And it would be if you had to cover it all in one big jump! But that's not the way you do it. You take one step at a time. Each step moves you closer to your goal, and *as long as you keep moving, you will reach the top*. Most people who fail to reach their goals do so because they don't do the first thing *first*. They don't put their feet on the first stair.

Short-term goals are where you begin. They can be exciting! They can change your life! They definitely will make you stronger, and they are easy if you take them one step at a time.

Jeff is a sophomore in high school. He might not be the best student, but he is a laugh a minute. Funny comments just seem to come out of his mouth no matter where he is.

At Jeff's school last November, it was decided that the students would present one play each semester to raise money for the student treasury. Posters went up encouraging student to try out for various parts in the comedy the student government had chosen to produce. Everyone suggested that Jeff try out for a part; he was always so funny, it seemed natural that he'd be a sure-fire hit.

But, thought Jeff, being funny in class is quite different from being funny on a stage with five hundred people watching! Jeff decided that he would be sick on the day of tryouts because he was sure that even if he got a part, he wouldn't be able to memorize his lines. He had never been any good at that sort of thing. Besides, who wants to look like a fool in front of the whole world?

Rehearsals began. From the beginning, it was clear to Mr. Garrett, the director, that one of the roles, the one with the funniest lines, had been miscast. A boy named Toby had the part, and everyone—including Toby—knew he was wrong for it.

With only three weeks left before the play was to open, Mr. Garrett knew that unless something were done with Toby's part, the play would be a flop. He had a talk with Toby; they discussed changes in the dialogue and actions. Finally, Toby looked at Mr. Garrett and said, "You and I both know what the problem is. I'm not right for this part. I don't look like the character is supposed to look, and I don't have the personality, either. I'm too serious. I know that you really wanted Jeff to have this part—and right now, I do too!"

Mr. Garrett told Toby to think it over and he would speak to Jeff about taking the part. If Jeff said no, Toby agreed that he would just do his best. When Mr. Garrett told Jeff about the conversation he'd had with Toby, Jeff turned pale. "Don't ask me to do this, Mr. Garrett. I can't memorize that much stuff."

After fifteen minutes of discussion, Mr. Garrett had Jeff calmed down enough to suggest a plan for learning the lines. "You have twenty days until the show opens. There are only ten pages of dialogue for you to learn. Let's break those pages down and we'll work together for the next ten days memorizing one page a day. When you are finished, you will still have ten days to rehearse. What do you say?"

Jeff agreed to give Mr. Garrett's plan a try.

Each day for the next ten days, Jeff knew that he had to memorize one page of lines. When he looked at all the dialogue together, the task seemed enormous, but when he thought only about one page—well, that seemd possible.

Each page contained twenty-two lines. Jeff promised himself that he would learn eleven lines before noon, and another eleven lines before five o'clock. His main goal was to do well in the performance. In order to do that, Mr. Garrett explained, he had to set these *daily* goals.

All Jeff thought about the first day were those twenty-two lines. He made believe that the twenty-two lines were all he ever had to do! He worked as hard as he could on just one page a day.

By the time the ten days were over, Jeff did, indeed, have every line committed to memory. In the remaining ten days, he rehearsed with the rest of the class and learned all his actions and cues.

Opening night arrived, and Jeff was ready for his performance. He was nervous, of course, but at the same time he was excited. He told Mr. Garrett how he felt and Mr. Garrett told him that he understood—he also said he hoped the two of them could have a talk after the run of the play was over.

It was fantastic! The play ran three nights, and each night, Jeff received more applause than any of the others in the cast.

When the curtain fell for the last time, Mr. Garrett smiled to himself and thought about the talk that he and Jeff would soon have. That conversation took place the following afternoon.

"Wow! Last night was incredible!" exclaimed Jeff. "I really like performing n front of all those people. Do you suppose I could become an actor, Mr. Garrett?"

"You did very well, Jeff. We're all proud of you. The play earned more money than we had planned, but I think you got something very special out of this whole experience. Do you know what it is?"

"I'm not sure. I just know that I feel different."

"Jeff, you're a bright kid with a quick mind, but you've never done anything on your own before. You were never willing to stretch yourself and see what you could do. You never committed yourself to anything—sports, grades, nothing.

"In order to learn your lines, you had to set a goal for yourself and work toward it. You didn't think that you could do it when you first heard about it. When we broke the manuscript down and set one page a day for your goal, the whole idea became possible in your mind. Do you understand?"

"Yeah. I think I do. Ten pages is way too much to learn . . . but to learn one page a day—even I could do that!"

Step by step. Jeff hadn't had to worry about Tuesday's lines until Tuesday morning. All he had to do on Monday was just take care of the twenty-two lines that were his responsibility that day. By the time Wednesday came, he had already learned forty-four lines.

Day by day. Step by step. One thing at a time. Before you realize it, you are at the top of the stairs, ready to claim your *earned* goal.

Deciding what you want

M aybe it's time for you to sit down and think about some of the things you would like to have happen to you now and in the future. Why not take a sheet of paper and a pen and go someplace where it's quiet. Make a list of things that you would like to accomplish and things that you would like to own. Don't bother putting them in order. The main thing is just get your dreams down on paper.

After you've finished your list, put it away for a few days and mull over the things you've listed. When you return to your list, choose *just one* of the things that you would like to achieve and draw a big circle around that one item. Next to that circle, write the date by which you would like to accomplish your goal.

Now take another sheet of paper and write a statement about the goal that you have chosen. You can start it like this:

More than *anything* in the world, I would like

_____

_____

_____

_____

I want to have reached my goal by _____
                                    (date)

Memorize what you've written. Repeat it to yourself throughout the day. Repeat it just before you go to sleep and *immediately* upon waking up each morning.

When you repeat your statement to yourself, believe with all your heart and mind and soul that your *desire* will become a *reality*. As you repeat your desire, try to picture yourself as already having reached your goal. It is important that you concentrate with all your power on how it will feel when you actually reach that goal. It is most important that you pretend that you are actually in possession of whatever it is that you want.

Be excited and determined when you say your statement over and over. Put all your feelings behind it! The enthusiasm and excitement you feel should come from the fact that you *know* that you are going to reach your goal.

Your goals don't always have to be for serious dreams. There's room in your life for some fun goals, too. You have every *right* to do happy things with your life! *You should be good to yourself and give yourself fun goals from time to time.*

Pam is a senior in high school. For the past couple

of years her family has been spending Easter vacations in the Bahamas, and Pam always enjoyed these trips to the warm islands. After their vacation during her junior year, Pam asked her parents if they would be willing to let her go there alone the following year.

After thinking about it for a long time, Pam's parents decided that Pam had always shown good judgment in the things she had done in school and at home. She obeyed the rules that they had given her and had never gotten into any serious trouble. (Pam isn't a goody-goody, she's just a person who uses good sense.)

Pam's parents told her that she could go, with the stipulations that she would have to find a girlfriend to go with her and she would have to pay for it all herself. Pam immediately began looking for someone to go with her.

Her friend Beth was interested in going, and Beth's parents said they would allow her to make the trip. Although it was almost a year ahead, Pam and Beth started making their plans. They went to travel agencies and asked for all the information they could find on flights, prices, and so forth, and they discussed all the different arrangements that were available.

When they had made up their minds about where they wanted to stay, they each had to give the travel agent a fifty-dollar deposit. Both girls knew that they had to pay for their own trips, so they made sure that they found jobs for the summer. They figured out how much it would cost, and drew up a budget so that they would know just how much they had to save each week.

In September, Beth told Pam that her plans had changed and she was unable to make the trip. Pam *immediately* started to look for someone else with whom she would enjoy her vacation.

A few days later, Pam found someone. Her name

was Gail, and although the two of them knew each other, they weren't what you would call good friends. Pam's parents went to see Gail's parents and they decided that Pam and Gail would be good traveling partners.

In November, the girls got a call from the travel agent saying that the air fares were going up and they would have to pay the entire amount of their tickets by the next day, or pay the increase. The money the girls would have to come up with turned out to be $200 each! Pam went to her father and explained what had happened and told him that she didn't have that much money. She did have a job, but it was only part time after school; she had *planned* on having more time to finish paying off the trip.

Pam's father told her that he would lend her the money, but he would need to have it paid back in three weeks. She agreed to do that, but she didn't at first see how she could, since her total pay for three weeks only came to about $150.

So Pam went to her boss and explained what had happened. She told him that she badly needed some extra money, and wondered if maybe he could use her for more hours a week. The man could see how determined she was and agreed to give her the extra hours she needed to earn the money.

Pam and Gail had their two-week vacation in the Bahamas, and returned looking great. They had wonderful tans and had really enjoyed themselves.

Now, let's take a look at what happened.

First of all, Pam had a *desire* to go on that trip. Picture her standing in her living room and announcing her desire. Her parents agreed, but they gave her some conditions that she had to follow: she had to find someone of whom they approved and she had to earn the money for her expenses, the clothes she would need, and the cost of the tickets and accommodations.

Pam never saw those demands of her parents as obstacles. She just knew that she wanted to go on that vacation, and she began to accomplish each step in an orderly fashion.

What happened when Beth dropped out of the picture? Pam could have said, "That rotten Beth! She wrecked everything! She planned to go and gave me her word and now she's changed her mind. My parents will never let me go without her!"

Pam *could* have said that, but she didn't. She just knew that she wanted to go on that trip! Her *desire* motivated her to look for another travel partner. And, of course, she found Gail.

The next problem was the $200 that she had needed sooner than she'd planned. That could have ended the whole plan right there, but it didn't. Pam borrowed the money from her father, and then went to her boss to see if she could set up a heavier work schedule that would allow her to make more money. She did it, too! Three weeks to the day after her dad gave her the money, she paid him back.

Many people fail to set *any* type of goal because they are afraid that they can't figure out the right way to reach their goals. They want something and they say that they are ready to work for it, but they never *go for it,* because they don't think that they are capable of laying out all the plans for themselves. They lack confidence.

Be different from these people. Make those plans for yourself and *make* them work. Just remember to do the *first* thing *first*. After that, all the other steps that are necessary for you to take to reach your goal will be obvious when the time is right to take them.

PAM'S STAIRWAY TO SUCCESS

LEAVES
FOR
VACATION!

INCREASES HOURS AT
WORK TO PAY LOAN
BACK IN THREE WEEKS

ASKS FATHER FOR LOAN TO
PAY OFF BALANCE OF BILL,
WHICH COMES DUE EARLY

FINDS ANOTHER TRAVEL
PARTNER WHEN FIRST GIRL
BACKS OUT

GOES BACK TO TRAVEL AGENCY TO LET
THEM KNOW WHICH PLAN THEY HAVE
CHOSEN AND TO PAY DEPOSIT

GETS A JOB TO PAY FOR ALL
TRAVEL AND PERSONAL EXPENSES

MAKES A BUDGET TO SEE HOW MUCH SHE WILL
HAVE TO SAVE EACH WEEK

PAM AND TRAVEL PARTNER DECIDE ON A TRAVEL
PACKAGE THAT IS RIGHT FOR THEM

GOES TO TRAVEL AGENCY TO GET INFORMATION
ON RATES AND ACCOMMODATIONS

LOOKS FOR AND
FINDS TRAVEL PARTNER

LISTENS TO THE CONDITIONS THAT HER PARENTS GIVE HER
(AND DECIDES TO FOLLOW THEM)

TALKS WITH
PARENTS

PAM ENTHUSIASTICALLY EXPRESSES HER DESIRE TO GO TO THE BAHAMAS
BY HERSELF

Start reading at the bottom of the stairs!

Take another look at Pam's vacation goal and the steps that she took to reach it. The following diagram should show you how logical each step was and the order in which they had to be taken.

You can see from the diagram that the steps that Pam took were in a *logical* order; she took them as they came. You can see that there were several unexpected steps. *Those are a part of every climb toward a goal!* When you get to those unforeseen steps, *don't* lose your balance or turn around. Just take that extra step!

You can also see from the diagram that Pam was not able to sit down at the beginning and diagram *exactly* what the steps would be that she would have to take. *It will be the same for you.* When you *decide* on your goal, don't be discouraged if you can't plan each and every thing along the way. *You will find that each step you need to take will be obvious when the time comes for you to take it.*

What happens to people who don't have goals?

W ithout long-term goals, people wander through life without a clear purpose or destination; frequently they arrange their lives to conform to other people's ideas of what they should do.

There are people without goals all over the world! They are the people who hate to get up in the morning. They are the ones who are working at jobs that are totally wrong for them. They are the unhappy, frustrated people whose days and years run together in a blur of indistinguishable time. One day is just like the next. These people are like robots.

Gary is a good example of a person without long-term goals. He was good looking and had a circle of friends who loved sports and good times. Gary and his friends weren't good enough athletically to be on any of the varsity teams because they couldn't stick to the rules about practice. They didn't try to maintain good grades, either. You could find this group of guys on the B teams and at *all* the parties every weekend. They spent their spare time planning their next entertainment.

When graduation time rolled around, the gang did graduate—every last one of them. None of them were on the honor roll, but they were out of school. They were so glad to be away from the routine of trying to get out of homework assignments that none of them gave any thought to going on to college. They were going to get jobs and have more fun!

Two of Gary's friends, Tom and Chris, got jobs at the plant where Chris's father worked. They started their jobs at the same time—the week after graduation. Gary couldn't find a job, and since he was still getting an allowance from his parents, he wasn't breaking his neck trying to find work.

After a couple of months on the job, Chris decided that he didn't like working at the factory and that he would join the army. When Chris told Gary about his decision, he added, "Hey, buddy, why don't you go and apply for my job. I know they're lookin' for somebody."

Gary said, "Why not! I'll go over there on Monday." Gary's father had been warning him that he should start to look for a job because his allowance was coming to an end, and Gary had decided that he had better look for something if he wanted to keep his car—and be able to afford gas for it.

Gary went to the plant on Monday morning and said that he wanted the job that his friend was leaving.

He filled out an application and was called in to work the following day. *Gary spent less time deciding on his job than he spent picking out a new shirt.*

At first the job was great—that is, the pay was good. He had enough money to have bigger parties and a bigger car. He bought a couple of pairs of new jeans, some new shirts, a stereo system, better speakers for his car. This was the life!

Gary continued to spend his time with "the guys." They all dated girls with the same attitudes that they had. They loved to have fun! Then one by one, the couples started to get married, and by the time they were twenty-four, everyone in the crowd was "hitched."

Tom was the first one to get married and the first one to become a father. It wasn't long before he and his wife moved into a new subdivision because they needed more room. Tom was still working at the plant, but he was discovering that the paycheck he brought home now had a lot more things to cover! "Babies and wives are expensive," he said to the rest of the gang one evening.

When Gary and his wife started their family, they had to look for a larger place to live, too. Gary mentioned to Tom that he was looking for a place and Tom said, "Listen, just down the block from us there's a place like ours for sale. Wouldn't it be great! We'd be living in the same neighborhood and our kids could be friends. Some of the other guys live in another subdivision next to ours."

How much more convincing do you think Gary needed? The following month Gary and his family moved into a house that was just like Tom's—and every other house for blocks around. The only difference was the color of the siding and the way the trees and shrubs were planted.

Meanwhile, Gary's paycheck no longer stretched

to include new jeans, shirts, and stereo systems. The only things it covered now were house payments, insurance, food, medicine, and trips to the doctor's office. There was never anything left over. But Gary stayed in his job because it was a job. "Heck!" he reasoned, "a lot of guys don't even have jobs. At least I have a place to go every day, right?"

Gary's job was easy. He did the same thing over and over a hundred times a day. There wasn't any way he could get a promotion because the man who owned the plant had all his relatives working for him in the management jobs, so why hustle? "No point in doing anything fancy, it isn't gonna make any difference anyway," Gary said. All his co-workers agreed.

Good-looking, middle-of-the-road Gary. He came home from work every night, fell into the chair nearest the television set, opened a beer, and night after night after night watched people who were making twenty times more a year than he. His world revolved around his special shows each week. On Friday night, there wasn't anything on that he liked, so he and his wife would go over to one of the other couple's homes and talk about work, the good old days, and how expensive it was to raise kids.

The years passed, the kids grew up and moved away, and suddenly Gary was sixty-five and it was time to retire. He was a grandfather now. One day while he was sitting in front of his television set, his eight-year-old grandson climbed up on his lap and said, "Grandpa, tell me all the exciting things you did in your life."

"Well," he said, "I . . . "

Are you going to plan for your future, or would you rather be like Gary? Gary's life wasn't really so bad. He had a job. He had a wife. And he had three children. So what if his job was boring and he never had the

money to take a vacation? So what if he never accomplished anything that he could tell his grandson about
with pride? He had kept a roof over their heads, hadn't
he? They had eaten, hadn't they? They still saw the
same faces every Friday night, didn't they? It wasn't so
bad.

If you want a life like Gary's, it won't be hard for
you to follow his path. To live that way, all you have to
do is refuse to set any goals. Refuse to set a destination.
Just take what comes along and you will soon find yourself living just like Gary—in a place called Dullife.
Dullife is a little town where nothing much happens.
It's a place with no excitement and no opportunities.
The people who live in Dullife watch life happen to
other people. They are just spectators.

If you want to be a *part* of life, instead of just a
spectator, you will have to spend more time deciding
on a job and your future than you spend picking out
what you are going to wear to school tomorrow.

What should I do if I don't know what I want to do in the future?

If you choose wisely, the time that you spend at your
job will be exciting and your work will contribute to
the happiness of your family and to the variety of your
social life. There are so many thousands of opportunities for you. Even the *process* of finding a job or a career
choice is exciting.

If you are currently in junior high or high school,
make an appointment with your counselor. Ask him or
her what resources are available at your school for career

advice. Most schools have catalogs, pamphlets, and other material that describes various jobs, vocations, and careers. These reference works will tell you how much education is required for a particular position, as well as give you information on the availability of jobs in a given field. You will also be able to learn what degree of income you can expect from the various jobs or careers.

If you live in an area where there is a community college or a four-year college, check to see if they have a career counseling service that is available to the public, or if they offer a course on career planning in which you can enroll.

Another source of information on career planning is the U.S. government. Every year it prints a book entitled *Occupational Outlook Handbook*. This book outlines the areas in which employment is available, describes the positions available within specific categories, and tells you where to look for further information on any given opportunity. To receive a copy, write to:

> Superintendent of Documents
> U.S. Printing Office
> Washington, D.C. 20402

Check with your local library. Most states produce occupational information and statistics pertaining to employment within the state. Also, ask the librarian at the reference desk to help you find the names and addresses of sources for information on career planning and development.

Whether you are in junior high, high school, college, or old enough to be a grandparent, career counseling and opportunity research is available to you. If you are already in a job or career you no longer enjoy, do something about it! It is never too soon, or too late, to change the direction of your life!

Don't depend on someone else to plan your future for you. Don't depend on someone else to provide an income for you. If you want independence and financial security, it's up to *you* to get them.

Your life is far too important to leave in someone else's care, and it's far, far too important to leave to chance.

When you take time—*plenty of time*—to think about the type of work that would provide you with satisfaction, the income level at which you could be comfortable, opportunities for advancement, and a geographic region that would suit you, *then take the first step* in the direction you want to go, there is no doubt that your future will be exactly what *you* want it to be.

- DREAMS BECOME REALITY THROUGH DESIRE.
- YOUR GOALS ARE LIKE DESTINATIONS ON YOUR JOURNEY THROUGH LIFE.
- SHORT-TERM GOALS PREPARE YOU FOR LIFE-TIME GOALS.
- ALL GOALS BEGIN WITH TAKING THE *FIRST* STEP *FIRST*.
- AS LONG AS YOU KEEP MOVING IN THE RIGHT DIRECTION, YOU WILL REACH YOUR GOAL.
- YOU CAN REACH ANY GOAL BY WORKING FOR IT ONE STEP AT A TIME.
- EACH STEP YOU NEED TO TAKE TO REACH YOUR GOAL WILL BECOME OBVIOUS WHEN THE TIME COMES FOR YOU TO TAKE IT.
- IT IS NEVER TOO EARLY OR TOO LATE TO THINK ABOUT YOUR FUTURE; OR TO CHANGE THE

DIRECTION OF YOUR LIFE.

➠ DON'T DEPEND ON SOMEONE ELSE TO PLAN YOUR FUTURE FOR YOU.

11

Value Your Time

Y ou can spend as much money as you earn, you can spend as much money as you are given, you can spend as much money as you can borrow—some people even spend as much money as they can steal—but you cannot spend your life by more than a second at a time. It doesn't matter whether you are the richest person who ever lived, or the poorest. Each of us lives only *one* second at a time.

Misused time is the greatest cause of unhappiness and failure

T he average life expectancy of a person born in the United States today is approximately seventy years. Let's pretend that from the time a person was twelve years old, he or she wasted only *five* minutes a day for the remaining fifty-eight years of his or her life. That may seem like a very small amount of time, but at the end of that person's life, the wasted time would add up to one fifth of a year, or 73½ days. That is a lot of time when you consider that those are twenty-four-hour days. A waste of five minutes per day for fifty-eight years adds up to a total of 1,764 hours. It's sad to consider that most of us waste a lot more than five minutes each day!

How much time do you waste in the average day? If it's a half hour and we multiply that by 58 years, at the end of your life, you will have thrown away 10,585 hours—or 441 complete days—more than a year and two months! Can you *imagine* the things you could do if you had that many free days? If you were to go to a four-year college, it would only take 2,400 hours of in-class time for you to fulfill your requirements for graduation. If you spent an additional 4,800 hours in study outside the classroom, your total hours would still only add up to 7,200. You would have 3,385 hours left. With those hours, you could be well on your way to a master's degree. All of this from only one half hour per day! It would be more than enough to change your entire life.

Imagine how well developed your ability to play the guitar would be with 10,585 hours of practice! Imagine how much you could learn about the solar system in 10,585 hours of study! Imagine how accurate your aim would be if you shot baskets for 10,585 hours! Imagine how many solutions you could discover for the problem of world hunger in 10,585 hours! Imagine what an impact you could make on the world with 10,585 hours of expressions of kindness to others! Imagine what you could gain in *any* endeavor with an investment of 10,585 hours!

Businesses don't become prosperous without financial budgets. People who have financial budgets are more economically successful than those who don't have them. You know what a financial budget is. You can make one for yourself by taking a piece of paper and drawing a line down the middle of the page from top to bottom. On one side, write down how much money you expect to have coming in during the next week; on the other, list the expenses that you *expect* to have for that week. For example:

Projected Income and Expenses for June 20–27

INCOME	EXPENSES	
$20	Tickets for concert	$ 4.00
	Repayment of loan to brother	3.00
	Donation for fire victims	2.00
	Gas for car	10.00
	Savings account	1.00
$20	TOTALS	$20.00

When you work out a budget and stick to it, you know where you are money-wise all the time—you can see where your money is coming from and where it is going, and you have greater control over it. Having a budget means that you plan *ahead of time;* you make your budget before you do any spending. If you haven't thought about future uses and obligations of your money and don't have a budget, it's very easy to spend it impulsively. You see a sweater that you just can't live without, or a new tape that you must have. You figure, "Why not? It's not *that* much money!" But taking a chunk of that cash without stopping to think could cause you some *big* problems in just a short time—such as when an emergency comes along or an opportunity to go someplace special crops up.

Time is more valuable than money—smart people invest their time wisely

S mart people *plan ahead*. Smart people plan their time just like they plan their money. *Time really is more valuable than money*. With money, if you discover that your expenses are averaging more than your income, you can always look for a better-paying job, or think of another way to earn more money. When you are ten years old, for example, ten dollars a week is a lot of money. When you are seventeen years old, ten dollars a week probably seems like nothing! The older we become, the greater our financial needs and obligations become. But, no matter how old you are, there are only twenty-four hours in your day. The older you become, the more hours you would like to have to accomplish all you want to accomplish. No matter how you may wish for an extra hour—or even an extra ten minutes—a day, the length of all our days will always stay the same—only twenty-four hours long.

You can do everything you want to do in one day *if* you make out a time budget for your day. Make your time budget just like your money budget—*before* you spend the time. Take a piece of paper and write the hours of the day along one side—and what you hope to do, or have to do, opposite those hours.

HOUR	ACTIVITY
Midnight	Sleep
1:00 A.M.	Sleep
2:00 A.M.	Sleep
3:00 A.M.	Sleep
4:00 A.M.	Sleep
5:00 A.M.	Sleep
6:00 A.M.	Sleep
7:00 A.M.	Get up, take shower, eat breakfast, straighten room
8:00 A.M.	Leave for school
9:00 A.M.	Class
10:00 A.M.	Class
11:00 A.M.	Class
Noon	Lunch with friends
1:00 P.M.	Class
2:00 P.M.	Class
3:00 P.M.	Go to work
4:00 P.M.	Work
5:00 P.M.	Go home. Start homework
6:00 P.M.	Have dinner
7:00 P.M.	Help with dishes
8:00 P.M.	Finish homework
9:00 P.M.	Watch television
10:00 P.M.	Get ready for bed and do tomorrow's budget
11:00 P.M.	Sleep

That's a pretty full day, isn't it? But if you didn't have this day planned ahead of time, it would be very easy to get home from work, have dinner, and plop yourself in front of the television set for a couple of hours. If you did, you would be forced to either give up some of your sleep hours or some of your homework hours. Either way, you would be the loser the next day. Once all the hours in a day have been spent, *you can't buy back even one second of it.*

With enough preparation, you can make room in your day for anything that you want to do or have to do. Successful people plan their days. That's one of the main reasons that they are successful.

Invest your time in your special interests

While you are in school, you are directed to follow a certain pattern of education. The school board, the administrators, and your teachers decide what fundamental courses should be taught. The basics that you learn while you are in school prepare you for life and help develop your interests for a job or for future study in college.

If you are interested in developing your imagination and creativity and are following the suggestions in the Use Your Imagination chapter, there will come a time when you are in class, watching television, listening to other people, reading a magazine or newspaper, or just plain daydreaming when you become fascinated with a subject that isn't fully covered in your curriculum. When that happens, you have a marvelous opportunity! In fact, *within that moment may just be the opportunity of your lifetime.*

By making a very small investment of your time, you can become *an expert on the subject* in which you are interested. All you need is thirty minutes each day to devote to it.

For example, let's pretend that the subject you are interested in learning more about is aqua-culture, also known as sea-farming. Why not try a thirty-day test to see just how much you are able to learn in this short time? Go to your nearest library, and begin by looking in the card catalog under "aqua-culture." Write down the titles and call numbers of the books you find with information on the subject, locate them, and check several out. (Don't hesitate to ask for help if you can't find what you are looking for, or if you don't know how to use the card catalog.) Once you have your reference books, begin by reading thirty minutes each day.

If you have read all the books on your subject before your thirty days are up, go back to the library and ask for the *Reader's Guide to Periodical Literature*. In this guide, under your subject, is a list of articles that have been published in magazines on almost any subject. You may need help in using the guide at first. Helping you find what you want is the librarian's job. Don't hesitate to ask for assistance.

Depending on the magazine, and how recent its publication, you may or may not be able to take it from the library. If you cannot take it with you, do your thirty minutes of reading right there at the library.

Now take a look at what's happening! First of all, you started with a subject you didn't know much about. Then you gave that subject thirty minutes a day for thirty days. Do you realize how much time you've invested? Fifteen hours! When you think about it, it doesn't seem like all that much time out of a whole month, does it? But look what you have learned in a month of only thirty minutes a day! Can you imagine how much you could learn about *one specific subject* if you were to continue your experiment for a whole year? From an investment of 182½ hours of study on one subject, you would have an impressive understanding of your topic.

If you find something that stimulates your interest, and you spend just a half hour each day developing your knowledge on the subject, you may very well be determining your choice of career or job. This interest may provide the answer to your special talent or ability.

➠ MISUSED TIME IS THE GREATEST CAUSE OF UNHAPPINESS AND FAILURE.

➠ SMART PEOPLE BUDGET THEIR TIME AS WELL AS THEIR MONEY.

➠ WHEN YOU PLAN AHEAD, YOU CAN MAKE TIME FOR ANYTHING YOU HAVE TO DO OR WANT TO DO.

➠ BECOME AN "EXPERT" ON SOMETHING THAT INTERESTS YOU WITH A THIRTY-MINUTE-A-DAY INVESTMENT.

➠ IF YOU WANT PERSONAL POWER, INVEST YOUR TIME IN ACQUIRING AND USING KNOWLEDGE.

12

Turning Points and New Beginnings

N
o matter how carefully you plan your journey through life, unexpected events will occur over which you have no control. These events may be serious enough that you will have to leave the road on which you have been traveling and find an alternate route. Depending on how serious the obstacle in your path, you may never be able to return to the original route you had chosen.

No one likes to think about obstacles and pain, but they are a part of life. If you can think of them in that way, instead of as a punishment of you personally, you will be much better able to face them when they do occur. Unexpected, unhappy events happen to *every-one*—not just to you. None of us can live through an entire lifetime without feeling sorrow and pain. There will be times when you are lonely, and there will be times when you fail. There may even come a time when you feel as though your whole world has fallen apart.

When someone you love dies; if you are in an accident and lose the use of some part of your body, if your parents tell you that they are getting a divorce; or when anything over which *you have no control* happens, *the best thing you can do is learn to accept it.* You can kick and scream; you can retreat into yourself and cut off your friends and family; you can run away and cause great anxiety and pain in everyone you leave behind; you can blame everyone else for your misfortune. None of these things will undo what has happened; *all they can do is waste your time and energy.*

When there is a crisis or tragedy in your life, the feeling of loneliness and isolation that stems from it is very real and very frightening. You can face it more easily if you will remember that everyone else in the world has experienced hardships of one kind or another during their lives. You aren't alone, even though you may feel that you are.

Because of the way our bodies and minds work, it isn't healthy for us to bottle up or suppress our feelings. The healing process can't begin until the emotions are spent. Most often, that starts with tears.

One of the greatest misconceptions is that tears are a sign of weakness. To deny anyone the comfort of tears is cruel! Crying is a cleansing and soothing experience. The hurt and pain that are the result of tragedy or crisis are released from our bodies in the form of tears. When you feel tears start to sting your eyelids, don't try to hold them back. If you feel more comfortable shedding them alone, then find a place to be alone; but don't feel that you *have* to hide. Don't feel that you can't show others that you hurt, or that you need comfort. It's okay to expose your need for comfort. It's *very* okay to cry.

As soon as you are able, *reach for help*. Depending on your individual crisis, there are resources to help you deal with your situation. No matter what has happened in your life, *you are not alone.* There are others who have experienced similar obstacles and who understand what you are going through; there *is* help for you.

Even if your particular problem isn't what you would consider an immediate emergency, you may *know* that you need to "talk it out" with someone who understands what you are experiencing. *Don't hesitate to ask for help* from your friends, a responsible adult, your family doctor, or any other person you feel you can trust to put you in touch with professional help or a support group.

If you were having trouble with your car and couldn't fix it yourself, you would surely know that just ignoring the trouble wouldn't make it go away! When you ignore a problem with your car, it leads to greater expense when you finally do have to take it in for repairs. If you ignore a mechanical problem long enough, your car will eventually break down altogether. The same is true for any warning signal that your body or mind gives you! When you *sense* that something isn't working properly, let someone trained in that area check things out. It will save you needless complications later.

Asking for help and searching for answers is not a sign of weakness; it is a sign of intelligence and strength.

Don't allow your hardships to become excuses for not trying

R emember the story about Bill? When he was a very young man, the highway on which he was traveling was permanently closed. He lost his legs. Do you recall the rest of the story? Bill found *another* road on which he could continue his journey. It was a different road, and surely a road that he would not have voluntarily chosen. He made the most of that road, though, didn't he?

David's story is a little different. David told his family that he wanted to be a doctor. He was only fourteen years old. His parents were very understanding and encouraging.

David's determination to become a doctor grew into an obsession. It was the only thing he thought about; his life revolved around his studies. He knew that his goal required the best he could do in school.

After David graduated from high school, he went to college. In his senior year he began applying to med schools. Even though David's grades had been very good in college and he had proved himself to be a well-rounded person by being involved in many activities, ten out of the eleven medical schools to which he applied turned him down.

One night late in his senior year, when David was at the lowest point in his life, he received a call from his parents. His mother, father, and sister were on three different phones at home. David knew that this call meant that something serious had happened. He could tell by the sound of their voices that he had better sit down. His father said, "Dave, your sister has something to tell you."

"Dave . . ." his sister said shakily, "you've been accepted at Temple."

Dave couldn't believe what he had heard, so he asked his sister to repeat the news. She said it again. "Dave, you've been accepted at Temple Medical School in Texas."

David was overcome with joy. He couldn't believe

it. His dream! His chance! He was going to be able to have his dream!

David went to Temple Medical School and did very well. Then he served his time as an intern. In June, 1976, at a ceremony he dreamed would happen, he accepted a parchment scroll that rechristened him David W. Hartman, M.D.

Are you wondering how this story fits into this chapter? Well, there is something you don't know about David. The road on which he had been traveling as a child came to a dead end when he was eight. At eight years of age, David Hartman became permanently and completely blind. That's a fact that David couldn't change. *He had to accept it.*

David didn't allow his handicap to become a permanent disability by using it as an excuse for not trying. Neither should you. No matter how many times you are stopped along your own highway, there *will* be alternate routes for the continuation of your journey.

If you can't find another route by yourself, stop and ask directions. There are people all across the continent of your life who will be able to help you. It's a waste of time to stay lost and feel miserable. Get directions as soon as you need them.

If your life goes into a stall, like a car on the highway, find someone to help you move it. Don't leave it where it can be damaged further!

- OBSTACLES ARE A PART OF LIFE.
- OBSTACLES ARE NONDISCRIMINATORY; THEY HAPPEN TO EVERYONE.
- WHEN SOMETHING HAPPENS THAT YOU CAN'T CHANGE, THE BEST THING YOU CAN DO IS ACCEPT IT.

➠ TEARS ARE A VERY VALUABLE PART OF THE HEALING PROCESS. THEY ARE NOT A SIGN OF WEAKNESS.

➠ NO MATTER WHAT HAPPENS TO YOU, YOU ARE NOT ALONE. HELP IS AVAILABLE WHEN YOU ARE READY TO REACH FOR IT.

➠ ASKING FOR HELP AND SEARCHING FOR ANSWERS IS A SIGN OF INTELLIGENCE AND STRENGTH.

➠ NEVER USE A HANDICAP AS AN EXCUSE FOR NOT TRYING.

➠ IF YOU CAN'T CONTINUE YOUR JOURNEY AS PLANNED, THERE ARE ALTERNATE ROUTES THAT YOU MAY CHOOSE.

13

Putting It All Together

G o find a mirror and stand in front of it. Take a good look at yourself. There's been a change in you since you began reading the first chapter of this book, hasn't there? There's confidence in your eyes and enthusiasm in your smile. You have the posture of a person who has begun to realize that the future is exciting and that it belongs entirely to you. Bravo! You *should* look and feel that way, because you have come to the point where you are ready to travel across the continent of your life; riding on your *own* wheels and *in the driver's seat. You are really in control of yourself and the rest of your life.* You've *earned* the pride you feel and you *deserve* the respect that will be reflected in the eyes of those who know you.

This chapter will show you how to keep your battery fully charged at all times. When you complete this lesson, you will have the power you need to take yourself wherever you want to go in life. While other people are trying to decide *if* they want to go and *where* they want to go, you and your car will be moving ahead at a brisk, invigorating pace.

In your handwriting, copy the information from the boxes on the following pages. If possible, write them on three by five index cards so that they won't tear easily.

A POSITIVE PERSON!

I make the best of situations I can't control. I change the things about myself that I feel need changing. I look for the good in people and experiences; and refuse to dwell on anything negative.

ENTHUSIASTIC!

Everything I do is important, so I give 120% of myself to all I do.

PERSISTENT!

I never leave a project...job...goal...
or assignment until it's completed.
I hang in there until it's the best
it can be.

IMAGINATIVE!

I look for new ways to do things.
I search for new ideas and analyze old
ones. I take time every day to just
think and let my mind run free.

LEARNING!

Knowledge is power . . . and I'm a powerful person! I take every opportunity to expand my knowledge and increase my mental wealth.

RESPONSIBLE!

I take good care of myself, the things I own, and my obligations. Others can count on me because I follow through.

GOALS!

I know what I want to accomplish this year, this month, this week, and this day. As I work on my goals, I can measure my improvement and growth.

MY APPRECIATION!

I always find creative ways to say thank you for the help and love I receive from others. I make the people I know feel important by the thoughtful way I treat them.

A BIG IMPORTANT IMAGE!

I walk, talk, think and <u>act</u> like a very important person because I AM A VERY IMPORTANT PERSON.

FLEXIBLE!

I have an open mind and am willing to listen to new ideas. I know that nothing stays the same forever, so I'm adaptable and ready to change when necessary.

PATIENT!

I never find fault with others. I always remember that I cannot change another person. The only person I have control over and can change is <u>myself</u>.

DO MY BEST!

I work smart and I work hard! By working this way, I'm doing myself a favor. I'm becoming the best I can be!

MY TIME!

I make good use of my time. Every day of my life is important . . . and I live every day to the fullest.

A SENSE OF HUMOR!

I never take myself or my problems too seriously. I'm able to laugh at myself and my mistakes. Even though I laugh at myself, I never make fun of others!

HEALTHY!

I sleep eight hours a night; exercise every day and only eat food that's good for me. Junk food turns me off! I respect my body...and I make choices that will bring only healthy results.

HONEST WITH MYSELF AND EVERYONE ELSE!

One of my very best qualities is my truthfulness. Through my honesty, I've earned the respect and admiration of others.

NEVER SETTLE FOR SECOND BEST!

I do my best in all I do. Only the best comes from me!

GOOD JUDGMENT!

I'm careful to think about my actions before I do them.

CHEERFUL!

I smile a lot and always find something positive to say. I like people . . . and I always do and say things that bring out the best in them.

GOOD COMMUNICATION!

I look for opportunities to speak in public and to write my thoughts and opinions on paper. I listen to people who speak well and I learn one new word every day.

NOT AFRAID TO FAIL!

I'm willing to try; willing to risk. The only way I can really fail is if I don't try.

NOT AFRAID TO BE DIFFERENT!

I'm a person who does things my own way. I'm proud to be me. I'm special. Self respect is part of my personality because I have my own values . . . and I live up to them.

OUTGOING!

I look forward to meeting new people and I encourage them to talk about themselves and their ideas. I encourage others to believe in themselves.

A GOOD LISTENER!

I pay close attention to what others say . . . because I know that I learn when I listen . . . not when I talk!

CURIOUS!

I ask questions that begin with "Who–What–Where–When–Why–Which–How, and If." These are questions that help me learn. I ask questions to gain information . . . not to be nosey.

COURTEOUS!

Whenever I'm with other people, I always pretend that I'm the host. I do my best to make others feel comfortable emotionally, mentally and physically.

COURAGEOUS!

When things get tough, I take a stand and fight for what I know is right and fair. I've never been . . . nor will I ever be . . . a coward.

VERSATILE!

I'm developing interests in many different areas, because I understand the importance of having a well-rounded personality. I'm developing new skills and searching for new fields of interest. I'm an exciting, interesting human being.

Once you have your cards completed, stack them in the order in which they appear. Then pick up the top card and put it where you will see it many times during the day. Each time you see it, read it. Read it aloud, if possible. Read it with *enthusiasm*.

Make a commitment to yourself as you read your card. Practice the suggestion on that card for seven days. At the end of the seventh day, take the card on which you were working and put it on the bottom of the stack. Take a new card off the top and repeat the procedure for seven days. Keep going until you have completed all twenty-eight cards. Then start all over again!

IF YOU FOLLOW THIS PROGRAM WEEK AFTER WEEK, YOU WILL BE ACQUIRING STRENGTHS THAT WILL HELP YOU IN ANYTHING YOU WANT TO DO AND BE FOR THE REST OF YOUR LIFE.

14

Take the Wheel

All the people whose stories you've read, all the men and women who have done great things, everyone who has been happy or loved or wealthy—all these people started out just exactly like you. They were born. And they came into this world with the same thing that you did—potential.

As you have traveled through the chapters of this book, you have been given the help you need to discover and develop your potential. More than likely, you still don't have a clear picture of exactly what all your talents are. Not to worry. If you read each chapter carefully and follow its suggestions, you will be moving in the right direction, and those talents and abilities will soon become clear to you.

You are headed for the top of the mountain, where all you can ever dream of is waiting for you. Don't ever be discouraged when you stumble; don't ever stop trying, even if you think you can't go another step. *Keep your attitude positive, believe in yourself, and don't ever give up.*

While you are heading for your goals, I'll be cheering you on every step of the way! I believe in you!

Now, *go for it!*